Encountering Christ in the Covenants:
An Introduction to Covenant Theology

Daniel W. McManigal

Monergism Books

Monergism Books PO Box 491 West Linn, OR 97068

www.monergismbooks.com

Copyright © 2013 Daniel W. McManigal

No part of this book may be reproduced, stored in retrieval system, or transmitted in any form of by any means- electronic, mechanical, photocopy, recording, or otherwise-except for brief quotations for the purpose of review of comment, without the prior permission of the publisher, Monergism Books, P.O. Box 491 West Linn, OR 97068.

"Unless otherwise indicated, all Scripture quotations are from The Holy Bible, English Standard Version® (ESV®), copyright © 2001 by Crossway, a publishing ministry of Good News Publishers. Used by permission. All rights reserved."

Italics within Scripture quotations indicate emphasis added.

Printed in the United States of America

Cover photo by Cyrus Read

Monergism Books
PO Box 491
West Linn, OR 97068

ISBN-10:0989313107
ISBN-13:978-0-9893131-0-0

To Jesus,
The captain of our salvation,
The mediator of a better covenant.
(Hebrews 2:10; 8:6)

Acknowledgments

God sent many people along the way to encourage me through the process of writing this book. First, I must say, "thank you" to my dear wife, Jill, for the loving support and gracious attitude as I poured time and energy into this project. I'd also like to thank my children, Caleb and Ellie, for reminding me that there is a time for work and a time for play. My parents, Wayne and Willa McManigal, also provided plenty of support and helpful suggestions as they looked over the various revisions of the manuscript.

Without question, I am deeply appreciative and thankful for Rev. Clayton Willis who has logged more hours on this project than he probably cares to remember. I don't think this book would have seen the light of day without him. A special thanks is due to Frode Jensen, a great friend, ruling elder, and grammarian who caught countless mistakes and offered many improvements. I am also indebted to Ocieanna Fleiss for her willingness to look over the manuscript. Her many editorial suggestions greatly enhanced the book.

I am grateful for the congregations of Grace Church (URCNA, Portland, OR), Grace URC (Kennewick, WA) and Westminster OPC (Monroe, WA) for allowing me to present the materials that made up the bulk of this book. Thanks to Jeremy Baker, Reverends David Thommen and David Inks for their insights and suggestions as we have discussed so many details of covenant theology. Finally, I wish to thank John Hendryx from Monergism.com for his interest in publishing this introduction to covenant theology.

CONTENTS

Introduction 1
   Why this book? 2
   What is a covenant? 3
   Summary 5
   Two kinds of covenants 6
   Typology 6

Chapter 1: The Covenant of Redemption: If God Be For Us 9
   The covenant of redemption: What does it mean? 9
   Ephesians one 11
   Hebrews ten 14

Chapter 2: The Covenants of Works and Grace: Do This and Live; Live and Do This 17
   Looking for the right destination 17
   Summary 24
   The serpent's subtlety 27
   Adam's dying 28

Chapter 3: The Covenant with Noah: Preserved for the Sake of Promise 34
   The covenant with Noah: What does it mean? 35
   The spread of sin 36
   Righteous and blameless 39
   The place of salvation is rejected by the world 42
   Re-creation 45
   The covenant of common grace and the coming of Christ 47

Chapter 4: The Abrahamic Covenant: A Place for Abraham's People 50
   Blessings through Abraham 52
   The Abrahamic covenant: offspring and land 54

Chapter 5: The Mosaic Covenant: The Need for a Covenant Keeper 63
   Dying words, living faith 63
   Why was there grace in the Mosaic covenant? 65
   Why was there works in the Mosaic covenant? 67
   Another Adam-like figure 68

A guide to gratitude 73
Typology 74
How does this covenant further the covenant of grace made to Abraham and Adam? 75

Chapter 6: The Davidic Covenant: The King Will Come 80
A king for the kingdom 80
What is the Davidic covenant? 80
Context 82
The progression of God's promises 82
Offspring 84
God's house 87
Throne 90
The covenant with David was and is about Christ 92
The progress of God's covenants 95

Chapter 7: The New Covenant: A Reason to Rejoice 97
A fractured existence 97
Judah's decline 97
The new covenant 98
Who is God making this covenant with? 99
Not like the old covenant 99
What is the newness of the new covenant? 101
Law on the heart 102
The Lord will be known 104
Abounding grace 106
Christ of the new covenant 106
Conclusion 107

Chapter 8: The Covenant Servant: Promises Kept 109
Things new and old 109
Covenants are about Christ because the Bible is about Christ 110
The story of God's salvation 114
Matthew's gospel of Exodus 116
As it was in the beginning 118

Chapter 9: Covenant Initiation: Baptism 121
The valley of decision 121
After darkness, light 124
Who is doing the speaking? 125
Infant baptism 127
Our true spiritual lineage 129
New Testament continuity 131

Baptized households 134
The logic of the kingdom of God 134

Chapter 10: Covenant Meal: The Lord's Supper 137
Who and why? 137
Covenant eating and drinking 138
Points of contact with the Lord's Supper 139
Summary 140
Bread from heaven 141
What does this bread of life do? 142
How do we eat of it? 143
From hillside to upper room 145
Connecting the old covenants to the new sign 145

Introduction

I am one of a growing number of individuals not raised in a Presbyterian or Reformed Church but who has come into this church later on. In God's providence, I learned about the sovereignty of God while attending a Christian University. I eventually came to embrace the five points of Calvinism. It was thrilling to learn that God sovereignly chose an elect people before the foundation of the world and ordained that Jesus Christ would be the redeemer of those elect people, brought to faith by the power of his word and Spirit, and kept for eternity in the enjoyment of the new heavens and earth. Having grown up in the church, I never heard the doctrines of grace explained plainly because my church did not believe the five points of Calvinism.

I wondered what else I might have missed along the way. I began rethinking the issues most American evangelicals are preoccupied with: worship, baptism, Israel, the church, eschatology (what is going to happen at the end of the age), and so forth. To my surprise, I eventually discovered that all of these diverse topics are in one way or another connected to biblical covenants. One could say that without biblical covenants, there is no foundation for such things. And yet, when we compare the number of books on covenant theology to books on eschatology, the scales are clearly tipped in one direction. It is obvious that the latter has captured the interest and the imagination of evangelical Christians. Look at the indexes of books on basic Bible doctrines and see how many pages are devoted to the covenants. And how about in the church, how many sermons have you heard on the covenants? I would guess not many. At best, there seems to be only a vague familiarity regarding the covenants among church members today. We know covenants are in the Bible, but we are not really sure how their unfolding informs us about the Bible's meaning.

Fast-forward twenty-five years. As a pastor, I am not at all surprised to get the same set of questions year after year; questions about baptism, Israel and the church, and which millennial view is the right one. Sooner or later the question comes, "So why does the Reformed Church make such a big deal about covenant theology?" The answer to that question will go a long way to answering the other questions. It is the question behind so many other questions that are raised.

My hope is that the book you hold in your hands will show you why covenant theology is a big deal. Looking at the Bible through the window of the covenants will give you a better understanding of the way God relates to his people and it will help give you a framework to fit in the other matters too.

Why this book?

This book grew out of an evening sermon series preached at Grace Church (URCNA) in Portland Oregon and a summer camp for Grace United Reformed Church, Kennewick, Washington. It is not meant to be an academic treatment of the topic; it is my pastoral attempt to teach the theology of the covenants to God's covenant people. If it achieves this goal for readers, it will be worth every stroke of the keyboard. My goal is to help people see how the covenants of the Bible unfold the plan and purpose of God for the world from Genesis to Revelation. Because of space constraints, I cannot treat every covenant found in the Bible, but instead we will hit the high points in order to get a bird's eye view of the big picture. In broad strokes, our outline follows:

1. Christ is the center and goal of covenant theology. Covenants are about Christ.
2. God created Adam and entered into a covenant with him.
3. As the first man, Adam represented the entire human race.
   > If Adam was faithful in this commitment, the entire human race would be blessed. If Adam disobeyed, the world would be cursed.
4. Adam violated the terms of the covenant. The result was that Adam and everyone after him were estranged from God.
5. The covenants that follow Adam's fall take up the way in which God reclaims the fallen people he has chosen, through his Son whom he has appointed, for the purposes of bringing them to the place he has prepared, to enjoy God forever.

This is the storyline of the Bible. The covenants tell this glorious story of the sovereign King and his royal subjects. It is an amazing story of a Sovereign who has been slighted and insulted by his people again and again and yet, in his unfathomable love, he continues to pour out his mercies upon them.

The covenants tell us about what Adam should have done. They tell us how the human race was ruined and then how God restores and brings to an even greater conclusion what was lost. The covenants tell us that the purposes of God in the opening chapters of our Bibles were not trashed. The covenants teach us that where the first Adam failed, the second Adam, Jesus, succeeds as the representative of God's chosen people. Remove the covenants from the Bible and you are left with ancient accounts of ancient people, without rhyme or reason, in a world where things continue to go wrong. The covenants reorient us to the truth that God has a plan for this world and for us who are in it. What was said of Assyria could be said of all the ways of the Lord. "The LORD of hosts has sworn: 'As I have planned, so shall it be, and as I have purposed, so shall it stand'" (Isa. 14:24).

What is a covenant?

"What is a covenant?" It is a good question and has been answered a number of different ways. That probably isn't what you wanted to hear. A definition of *covenant* must be gathered from the places in which covenants are found. To be sure, some definitions of *covenant* are so in depth that they are too technical to be helpful for the person in the pew. Other definitions are intentionally broad but end up being less than helpful because they say very little about a great many things. I readily confess that I do not have a one-sentence definition that adequately captures what the word *covenant* conveys. What I do have is a very short list of definitions that will give you a flavor of what many in the Reformed tradition understand the covenants to be.

The first is taken from the Westminster Confession of Faith, chapter 7.1:

> The distance between God and the creature is so great that although reasonable creatures do owe obedience unto Him as their Creator, yet they could never have any fruition of Him as their blessedness and reward but by some voluntary condescension on God's part, which He has been pleased to express by way of covenant.

Moving from comma to comma, let's try to crystallize the main points. The first sentence teaches very plainly that there is a distinction between the Creator and the creature. The Creator stands over the creature as the Sovereign. The second sentence tells us that we will always owe loyal obedience to the Creator. In the third place there are both blessedness *and* reward. And that blessedness will never be ours unless God comes and bestows it through this relationship described as *covenant*. As a general rule, covenants between God and man are top down. God makes them; man receives them (Jeremiah 34 is a notable exception). If mankind is to have any enjoyment of God, God must come and tell his creatures how we are to live before him in this relationship and so be blessed by him. God always deals with his creatures through covenant.

Michael Horton wrote a book called *The God of Promise*. He writes, "A covenant is a relationship of oaths and bonds and involves mutual, though not necessarily equal commitments."¹ The covenant is not a casual relationship. Oaths ought to be kept; bonds should not be broken as the two parties live and act with integrity in the relationship they have committed themselves to. It is a relationship, but the relational does not negate the legal. The covenant is a relationship that is solemn and binding upon the parties who have committed themselves to one another.

In his book *The Christ of the Covenants*, O. Palmer Robertson said, "A covenant is a bond in blood, sovereignly administered."² By using the language of "bond in blood" Robertson is referring to ultimate things; these are life and death matters that this bond with the Lord creates. By adding that covenants are sovereignly administered, Robertson is also highlighting the concept that there is no bargaining with this Lord of the covenants. He brings the terms and conditions. He is sovereign and his subjects are to bow before his sovereign majesty with heart, mouth, and life.

In 1968 Meredith Kline wrote a book called *By Oath Consigned*.³ He has proposed the following definition. He writes, "In general, then, a covenant may be defined as a relationship under sanctions."⁴ What comes to your mind when you think of sanctions? The first thing that comes to my mind is a negative action imposed by an entity like the United Nations. Sanctions are negative things, such as the withholding of aid to countries that refuse to comply with UN decisions. For Meredith Kline, this really does not capture the biblical notion of sanctions in the Bible. Biblical sanctions cover both negative and positive outcomes of a relationship. There are positive sanctions and negative sanctions, or to use the biblical words, there are blessings and there are curses attached to this relationship that God has established with his people.

Finally, C John Collins explains that a biblical covenant, "…formally binds the parties together in a relationship; they are to be true to the covenant by keeping their promises of loyalty and commitment. There will be consequences for keeping or not keeping the covenant (benefits or punishments).⁵

---

[1] Michael Horton, *God of Promise* (Grand Rapids: Baker; 2006), 10.

[2] O. Palmer Robertson, *The Christ of the Covenants* (Phillipsburg: P&R, 1980), 15.

[3] Unfortunately it is out of print, but a pdf version can be found on the web (http://meredithkline.com/?page_id=37)

[4] M.G. Kline, *By Oath Consigned* (Grand Rapids: Eerdmans, 1968), 16.

[5] C. John Collins, *Genesis 1-4: A Linguistic, Literary, and Theological Commentary* (Philipsburg: P & R, 2005), 113.

Introduction

Summary

If your head is having a hard time grasping the various nuances that Reformed theologians have made, perhaps an illustration out of our own experience will help. You probably have lots of relationships with other people, but I would guess you don't swear oaths to those people. Though most of our relationships are casual, the marriage relationship might help us in our thinking about covenants.

When a man and a woman come together for marriage, they are entering into a covenant with each other. In fact, the Bible calls marriage a covenant (Mal. 2:14). When the man and woman come together there is usually a statement of intent, "Will you have this man/woman to be your lawfully wedded husband/wife…?" In the wedding ceremony vows are made, "I promise before God and these witnesses to love and to cherish, to have and to hold, in sickness and in health… till death do us part." Despite our culture's frivolous treatment of marriage, this vow is a solemn commitment. It is one man and one woman who belong to each other for life. Signs and seals of this relationship are given in the form of wedding rings and the relationship is established. The two are now one flesh. They are united to one another in the bond of holy matrimony. Things will go well or not so well depending upon their faithfulness to all that they have promised each other.

Like most illustrations this one breaks down, particularly when sin enters into the world because of Adam's transgression. Because Adam was created in God's image in knowledge, righteousness, and holiness (Eph. 4:24), he had the ability to give his word and be faithful to his word. Once he sinned, Adam could have sworn all he wanted to be faithful, but he didn't have the ability to keep his promises. But God made another covenant with him anyway. The Lord graciously promised to deliver Adam and his elect offspring. If we compare this with the example of a marriage covenant, it would be like God coming to his bride/people and declaring his intent to have them to be his own. God makes a solemn vow to commit himself to his people for their eternal good and he gives them his signs as pledges and seals of this relationship (Gen. 17:10; Ex. 12:11; Matt. 26:26-28; 28:19). Before the fall Adam had the ability to be faithful to all that God commanded him. After the fall, only God could faithfully accomplish every word of promise throughout the duration of the relationship.

The relationship was restored, but it was restored under different conditions, conditions that God would keep because Adam no longer could. The relationship is either one of perfect mutual fidelity between the two parties, or it is one of grace bestowed upon the offending party.

Theologians have tended to talk about these two covenant arrangements as the covenant of works and the covenant of grace.

Two kinds of covenants

The covenants between God and man basically fall under these two categories of works or grace (see the definitions below). You won't find the words *covenant of works* or *covenant of grace* in the Bible. But then again neither will you find the words *trinity*, *total depravity*, or *visible church/invisible church*. These concepts are everywhere in the Bible even though the specific words are not. Here we just want to introduce these two types of covenants, and we will explore them as we go throughout this study.

The Westminster Confession of Faith gives us nice summaries of these two kinds of covenants:

> The first covenant made with man was a covenant of works, wherein life was promised to Adam, and in him to his posterity, upon condition of perfect and personal obedience.[6]

> Man, by his fall, having made himself incapable of life by that covenant, the Lord was pleased to make a second, commonly called the covenant of grace, whereby He freely offereth unto sinners life and salvation by Jesus Christ, requiring of them faith in Him, that they may be saved; and promising to give unto all those that are ordained unto eternal life His Holy Spirit, to make them willing, and able to believe.[7]

In the pages of the Bible there are these two basic types of covenants. In the Covenant of works, God and man have a relationship where man has a duty to perform for a wage to earn, namely eternal life. In the covenant of grace, God and man have a relationship where God promises to perform the duty of giving man eternal life.

Typology

As I will go on to explain, God establishes both kinds of covenants, works and grace, in order to reveal his purposes for his people and to show us the greatness of his son. As the covenants of the Bible unfold, they give clearer pictures of how God is going to bring his people to glory through Jesus. You have probably come across numerous prophesies in the Old Testament that point to the coming Messiah (Gen. 3:15; Deut. 18:15-19; Pss. 2; 110; Isa. 9:6-7; Zech. 6:12-13). In the Old

---

[6] Westminster Confession of Faith 7.2.
[7] Westminster Confession of Faith 7.3.

Testament there is more than just a prophetic word about the person and work of Christ. God used words and he used people, things and events to point to Christ. Old Testament prophesies announced it and Old Testament people and events foreshadowed what the Messiah would come to do. Adam, Noah, Moses, Aaron, Israel, and David foreshadowed a greater prophet, priest, king, and Savior. Even Israel's history pointed beyond Israel to the faithful life of the Son of God.

God imbedded reminders and signs in Old Testament history of the Savior. As Dennis Johnson describes:

> The performance of every covenantal mediator and participant- patriarch, prophet, priest, judge, king, husband, father, son, parents, children, servant- ultimately is to be interpreted in light of the ways it reflects (or falls short of reflecting) the perfect covenant obedience to be offered by Jesus.[8]

God used his people as well as their circumstances and situations to point to Christ. The exodus from Egypt was a historical event and it was a type of an even greater exodus. At the transfiguration, Jesus, Moses, and Elijah were talking about his departure, his exodus (Lk. 9:31). The exodus was an event that caused the people of God to look and long for their greater deliverance from Satan, sin, death, and hell. Only Jesus could secure this kind of salvation. Again Johnson writes:

> The biblical understanding of history is not cyclical but linear. Thus the element of resemblance or similarity that is highlighted when the New Testament interprets an Old Testament event, person, or institution as a *typos* [type] - a preview pattern of Christ and his redemptive work-is not based on the perspective of the common cliché, 'history repeats itself.' Rather, history has a direction. It is moving toward a specific goal, the triumph of God and the universal acknowledgment of the kingship of God.[9]

What this means, then, is that we should expect to uncover a deeper level of meaning in the biblical text than the historical circumstances it records. Our reading of the Old Testament isn't complete until we have seen the way in which the people and the issues that they faced pointed forward to God's solution, in his son. This typological reading of Scripture is not a mystical, secret way of interpreting the Bible because the New Testament writers interpret the Old in a Christ-centered way

---

[8]Dennis E. Johnson, *Him We Proclaim: Preaching Christ from All the Scriptures* (Philipsburg, NJ: Presbyterian and Reformed, 2007), 216.

[9] Johnson, *Him We Proclaim*, 226.

(Lk. 24:27; Rom. 5:14; Heb. 10:19-20).[10] As Jesus said of Moses, "He wrote about me" (Jn. 5:46). This means that we will discover Christ in the covenants. His shadow is cast in every covenant (Col. 2:17), from the time of Adam in the Garden of Eden, to the new covenant of Jeremiah 31. The obedience and success of God's people carried in them a forecast of the greater righteousness of the Messiah. The disobedience and failures of the saints of old reminded them of their need for one who would bear their sins and so turn aside God's wrath and condemnation. These types and shadows of Christ, embedded into the history of God's covenant people, were used to turn the heart of faith toward the God who justifies. As we listen to what Scripture has to say about Adam, Noah, Abraham, Israel, David, and Jeremiah, we will hear about Christ.

In conclusion, God's word teaches us that the Sovereign Lord condescended to his human creatures and established a covenantal relationship with his people. There are certain obligations to be performed, and there is a glorious future to be enjoyed through the work of Jesus Christ, our covenant-keeping mediator of the covenant, and the guarantee of the good things to come. This covenant relationship between God and his people is an ancient and vital relationship that continues to this very day. As you read, you do so as one who is in covenant with the good, all-wise, ever-present, loving God who is committed to bringing you to himself through his Son. Praise God for his covenants; covenants he keeps!

---

[10] For an example of this kind of typological reading of the Old Testament see chapter 8.

Chapter 1: The Covenant of Redemption: If God Be For Us

> Whereupon there was a special covenant, or mutual agreement made between God and Christ, as is expressed (Isa. 53:10), that if Christ would make himself a sacrifice for sin, then he should 'see his seed, he should prolong his days, and the pleasure of the Lord should prosper by him.'[1]

> If God had a name, what would it be
> And would you call it to his face
> If you were faced with him in all his glory
> What would you ask if you had just one question…
>
> What if God was one of us…
> Just a stranger on the bus
> Trying to make his way home.

In her 1995 hit song, "What if God Was One of Us," Joan Osborne mused over what it would be like if she "bumped into God" as he was trying to make his way home. God has a name (Ex. 3:13-15) and he did become one of us (Gal. 4:4; Heb. 4:15). His glory was revealed (Jn. 1:14) and will be more fully revealed on the last day (Isa. 66:18; John 17:24). He came for a purpose and when that purpose was achieved, he returned "home" (Acts 1:9; Jn. 14:1-3; Rev. 5:6). What brought the Son of God to the point of taking upon himself a human body and soul, and entering into human existence is the story of covenant theology, particularly the covenant of redemption.

The covenant of redemption: What does it mean?

The covenant of redemption is the basis upon which the covenants unfold in the Bible. The major covenants of the Bible are the outworking

---

[1] Edward Fisher, *The Marrow of Modern Divinity* (Ross-shire, Scotland: Christian Focus Publications, 2009), 64.

of this one covenant made between the members of the Godhead.[2] Michael Horton writes, "The covenant of redemption... is an eternal pact between the persons of the Trinity. The Father elects a people in the Son as their mediator to be brought to saving faith through the Spirit."[3]

Remember that there are two kinds of covenants, works and grace. What kind of covenant is this pact of salvation? When Jesus entered into this covenant of redemption, he was taking upon himself the obligations of the covenant of works. The covenant that the Father made with the Son was a covenant of works wherein a people were promised to Jesus upon condition of perfect and personal obedience. And Jesus, the righteous Son of God, fulfilled all of the terms and conditions laid down by his Father. As R. C. Sproul has put it:

> Jesus is the first person to get into heaven by His good works. We also get into heaven by good works—the good works of Jesus. They become "our" good works when we receive Christ by faith. When we put our faith in Christ, God credits the good works of Christ to our account.[4]

The covenant of redemption was a works covenant for Jesus for the purposes of bringing glory to God's name by saving God's people. God did not decree your salvation without a plan to save you, and that is really what the covenant of redemption is all about. There are no hypothetical plans to send the Son to pay for sins in general making the way of salvation possible. As the Synod of Dort declared, "And as God Himself is most wise, unchangeable, omniscient and omnipotent, so the election made by Him can neither be interrupted nor changed, recalled or annulled; neither can the elect be cast away, nor their number diminished."[5]

While the words *covenant of redemption* are not found in the Bible, many Reformed theologians are persuaded that the concept is. We do not have any verses that say in so many words, God the Father, Son, and Holy Spirit covenanted together in eternity. Nevertheless, our salvation makes good sense in light of a covenant or pact established by those who

---

[2] Sometime this arrangement is called the *Pactum Salutis* which is Latin for "the pact of salvation."

[3] Michael Horton, *God of Promise* (Grand Rapids: Baker; 2006), 78.

[4] R. C. Sproul, *Essential Truths of the Christian Faith* (Wheaton: Tyndale House, 1992), 66.

[5] Canons of Dort 1.11. The Synod of Dort met in the city of Dortrecht to deal with the teaching of Arminianism that were spreading in some of the Reformed Churches.

save. Charles Hodge, the great Princeton theologian of the twentieth century put it this way:

> When one person assigns a stipulated work to another person with the promise of a reward upon the condition of the performance of that work, there is a covenant. Nothing can be plainer than that all this is true in relation to the Father and the Son. The Father gave the Son a work to do: he sent Him into the world to perform it, and promised Him a great reward when the work was accomplished. Such is the constant representation of the Scriptures. We have, therefore, the contracting parties, the promise, and the condition. These are the essential elements of the covenant.[6]

Following Hodge's summary, let's look at several texts which help us to better understand what the terms and conditions of this covenant were.

Ephesians one

This first chapter of Paul's letter to the Ephesians shows us God's plan of redemption, a plan that Paul says was put in place before the foundation of the world. In eternity, the members of the Godhead were committing themselves to certain activities.

The apostolic greeting begins with God "our Father." In vv. 3-14 he shows us how that reality came to be. It is God the Father who blessed us with every spiritual blessing (v. 3). Knowing that Adam plunges himself and us into sin, how can anyone receive the blessings of God? What things must we do to receive God's blessing? Well, the answer is that we can do nothing; it rests not on our choice to please God, but on the good pleasures of God who chose us. Paul goes on:

> Even as he chose us in him before the foundation of the world,
> that we should be holy and blameless before him. (Eph. 1:4)

Now the question is who is the *he* and who is the *him*? "He chose us in him..." Paul began with the Father and spoke of our being blessed in Christ; therefore, we can draw the conclusion that the *he* refers to the subject of v. 3, namely God the Father. The *he* cannot be the Son because the phrase "chose us in him" is a parallel expression to the statement found in v. 3, "blessed us in Christ." The *he* is the Father. Our first conclusion is that God the Father blesses us and God the Father chooses us.

---

[6] Charles Hodge, *Systematic Theology*, 3 vols. (Grand Rapids: Eerdmans; 1997) 2:360.

We read a little further and we find another personal pronoun, "in love he predestined us for adoption through Jesus Christ..." (vv. 4-5) The Father is the one who predestines. That word *predestination* is the Greek word *proorizō*, which can mean to "decide from the beginning," or "set apart from beforehand." What Paul describes is the way in which God the Father set you apart from the very beginning. That is a remarkable thought. Why would he do that? We have the ground of this predestination at the end of v. 5, it is "according to the purpose of his will." And according to v. 6, what does God's will result in? It results in our "praise of his glorious grace."

First conclusion: God the Father blesses us, and God the Father chooses us.

Second conclusion: The Father decides from the beginning, and the Father makes his decision according to his will. And this is to the praise of the Father's glorious grace.[7]

But how will the Father's will be carried out? According to v. 4, God has orchestrated the plan before the creation of the world, and it is the Lord Jesus Christ who carries out this plan of his Father.

Follow the verses again: the Father has blessed us "in Christ" (v. 3). He chose us "in him" that is *in Christ* (v. 4). The Father has set us apart for adoption through Jesus Christ (v. 5) and we are blessed in the Beloved—that is to the one God loves, namely Christ (v. 6). In eternity the Father chose a people, a plan, and charged his Son to carry it out. What did the plan entail for the Son?

> In him we have redemption through his blood, the forgiveness of our trespasses, according to the riches of his grace. (Eph. 1:7)

It was God's plan to redeem his elect through the death of his Son. The crowning act of Christ's obedience to his father was his sacrifice upon the cross. It was a covenant unto death that we might receive life. Now what can we say about the Holy Spirit? Was the Spirit also a part of this eternal pact or agreement between the Father and the Son?

> [13] In him you also, when you heard the word of truth, the gospel of your salvation, and believed in him, were sealed

---

[7] Calvinism has sometimes been caricatured as a cold, sterile or even "dead orthodoxy." Yet the predestinating purposes of God ought to create a lively response in his undeserving people. As the first question of the Westminster Shorter Catechism asks: What is the chief end of man? Man's chief end is to glorify God and to *enjoy* him forever. (Emphasis mine)

> with the promised Holy Spirit, [14] who is the guarantee of our inheritance until we acquire possession of it, to the praise of his glory. (Eph. 1:13-14)

When the gospel came to you, it came with the Spirit who had been promised long ago. Your reception of the gospel by the power of the Holy Spirit is a fulfillment of Old Testament prophecy. The prophets spoke of a time when God would pour out His Spirit on all flesh (Num. 11:29; Joel 2:28). Christ Jesus also told his disciples to wait in Jerusalem until the promise of the Father was given (Acts 1:8). In the covenant of redemption, the Father's will was carried out by Christ and continues to be carried out by the Holy Spirit.

The covenant of redemption shows us the Christ-centered and Spirit-applied character of our salvation. Paul takes us back through the past and into eternity to show us the glory of all three members of the Godhead caring for us. It is a comforting thought for the child of God, and it can also be used to counter erroneous ways of thinking. For instance, have you ever met someone troubled over the thought of losing his or her salvation? Can salvation be lost (a common, but strange way to word it; as if salvation were like car keys)? Can a believer lose the Holy Spirit? If you think this isn't a Christian concern, just ask a pastor or try googling the question. There are well-meaning saints who fear their salvation has been lost because the Holy Spirit has left them. The covenant of redemption assures us this could never be the case. God has a plan: The Father elects a people. The Son, in turn, is sent to earn the salvation of his people by obeying God's law perfectly and by laying down his life on the cross. Christ has fulfilled the terms of his Father's will and has sealed the covenant in his blood. In return, the Father rewards the Son's obedience by granting salvation to the elect. Because Christ has been faithful to the plan of the Father, the Father sends the Spirit of God to apply Christ's work of redemption through the appointed means of grace--word and sacrament.

If the Spirit ever could be withdrawn from the believer, it would render Christ's death insufficient to save. If Christians could lose their salvation, it would, at least, suggest that the Father's plan was incapable of being carried out. If that were the case, then the praise of his glory would be muted.

The covenant of redemption is a comfort to Christians. From first to last it is God who decrees our salvation, carries out our salvation, and brings us into that salvation (1 Pet. 1:5). It provides comfort and encouragement knowing that all three members of the Godhead have been faithful to carry out the plan to redeem us for their very own.

Hebrews ten

In Hebrews 10 we find additional support that this arrangement in eternity was covenantal by having terms and conditions prescribed and carried out. In Hebrews 10:5-10, we have a commentary on the fortieth psalm:

> [5] Consequently, when Christ came into the world, he said,
>
> "Sacrifices and offerings you have not desired,
>   but a body have you prepared for me;
> [6] in burnt offerings and sin offerings
>   you have taken no pleasure.
> [7] Then I said, 'Behold, I have come to do your will, O God,
>   as it is written of me in the scroll of the book.'"
>
> [8] When he said above, "You have neither desired nor taken pleasure in sacrifices and offerings and burnt offerings and sin offerings" (these are offered according to the law), [9] then he added, "Behold, I have come to do your will." He does away with the first in order to establish the second. [10] And by that will we have been sanctified through the offering of the body of Jesus Christ once for all. (Heb. 10:5-10)

The psalmist was prophesying about Christ (v. 5), and Christ was coming to do the Father's will (v. 7). He was coming to implement the Father's purpose and carry out the Father's plan. What is the purpose of the Father according to v. 10? It is our sanctification, our being made holy.[8] How is the Father's plan for our sanctification carried out? Through the offering of the body of Christ (v. 10). It is the Father's will, carried out by Christ and applied to the believer by the Holy Spirit (cf. 1 Cor. 6:11; 2 Thess. 2:13) for our sanctification. The covenant of redemption not only has our salvation as its goal, but also achieves our holiness before God by giving us the holiness of Christ.

We talk a great deal about the progressive nature of sanctification which is that gradual renewing of the image of God in his people. It is a

---

[8] The Westminster Larger Catechism asks: What is sanctification? Sanctification is a work of God's grace, whereby they whom God hath, before the foundation of the world, chosen to be holy, are in time, through the powerful operation of his Spirit applying the death and resurrection of Christ unto them, renewed in their whole man after the image of God; having the seeds of repentance unto life, and all other saving graces, put into their hearts, and those graces so stirred up, increased and strengthened, as that they more and more die unto sin, and rise unto newness of life.

wonderful thing and even more wonderful in light of what lies in the past. No, I did not mean in the future, but in the past. There is a conformity to God's image that continues throughout this life, but there is also a complete sanctification that has already been accomplished. It is as if we are becoming what we already are. The definitive character of our holiness is stated as a past action. "And by that will we *have been sanctified* (v. 10, emphasis mine). The Greek verb *hagiazō* is in the perfect, passive tense which is another way of saying that this is a completed action.

Christ fulfills the terms of His Father's will and that means: 1. We have been set apart as sacred unto God. 2. We have been consecrated. 3. We have been made holy. Even as we experience this ongoing renewal, the final outcome of holiness has already been determined, agreed upon in eternity and carried out on our behalf by Christ in history.

In his earthly ministry, Christ often spoke of having a work from his Father to do. He must finish the work his Father had given him (Jn. 4:34). Jesus came down from heaven not to do his own will, but the will of the Father (Jn. 6:38). Jesus came to do the works of the one who sent him (Jn. 9:4). Toward the end of his ministry Jesus could say, "I have finished the work which you have given me to do" (Jn. 17:4; NKJV). He spoke of his Father giving him a people that could never be snatched out of the hand of God (Jn. 10:29). He spoke of the condition laid upon him—he must lay down his life for his sheep (Jn. 10:18). Then on the cross of defeat came the cry of victory, "It is finished" (Jn. 19:30). All the terms and conditions of the covenant of redemption had been satisfied. Redemption was secured.

Having entered into the covenant of redemption with his father in eternity, Jesus came to earth to undergo the covenant of works so that his people would be saved. All for whom Christ lived and died have a glorious future because of this eternal pact, this covenant of redemption. Before the foundation of the world, Jesus was assigned a kingdom (Lk. 22:29). A body was prepared for him as he came into this world determined to do God's will (Heb. 10:5-7). God's counsel and purpose are eternal; (Isa. 46:10; Ps. 33:11) therefore, God gave his servant-son to be a covenant for his people (Isa. 42:6). This Son was foreordained before the foundation of the world, (1 Pet. 1:20) and he will not fail to make you a child of the king and an heir according to the divine promise. While we are suspicious when people say it, in this case it is true that the members of the Godhead had your best (and greatest) interest in mind when they covenanted to save you.

The covenant of redemption also proves that God was not taken by surprise when Adam took a different path. Long before Adam represented us, God had appointed another representative. Christ the mediator, being fully God and fully man, was appointed approved and sent to reconcile man to God. "He stood," as Turretin so succinctly put it, "between the parties at variance."[9] He removed the barrier that separated us from God, he ended the hostility, he set the captives free, he silenced the opposition, he atoned for sins committed, he covered our shame, he provided us his righteousness, he earned what had been forfeited, and he gained the victory. As we look at the covenants, I hope you will grow in love and appreciation for your covenant-making and covenant-keeping Lord, who has forged this bond of love with you.

Study Questions:

1. What is the goal of the covenant of redemption?
2. Who are the parties of this covenant?
3. What role does each member play?
4. How can the covenant of redemption provide comfort to the Christian?

---

[9] Francis Turretin, *Institutes of Elenctic Theology*, 3 vols. (Philipsburg, NJ: Presbyterian & Reformed, 1994), 2:179.

Chapter 2: The Covenants of Works and Grace: Do This and Live; Live and Do This

Looking for the right destination

We knew we had to get on the train, but my wife and I could not read Japanese and the Tokyo train station is... well, let's just say it is complex. We finally managed to flag down a man who looked at our tickets, took pity on us, and motioned with his hand to follow him quickly. We had no choice. He was holding our train tickets. We were in the wrong part of the station, and we had to run if we were going to catch our train. Winded and out of breath, we made it just in time. We sat down in our seats, and a few moments later the train began to move. We were on our way to see my cousin in Northern Japan, or so we thought. An American was walking through the train and seeing us she asked where we were going. After telling her, she informed us that the train disconnects and different sections of the train go in different directions. We were once again in the wrong place, soon to be headed in the wrong direction and to the wrong destination. We did finally make it, but it took a lot of work to get there.

Where are you going and how do you get there? If you don't know the answer to those questions, then you are bound to get lost. Genesis 1-3 actually hints at the answers to those questions. Genesis 1-3 is not only about our origin; it is also about our final destiny.

Where is Adam going and how does he get there? That question has to do with the covenant of works. The Westminster Assembly described the covenant of works this way:

> The first covenant made with man was a covenant of works, wherein life was promised to Adam, and in him to his posterity, upon condition of perfect and personal obedience.[1]

The Belgic Confession does something similar, calling the command that God gave to Adam, "the commandment of life."[2] The Westminster Confession has a footnote referencing Genesis 2:17. That verse is the point where God makes a covenant with Adam, "but of the Tree of the

---

[1] Westminster Confession of Faith 7.2.
[2] Belgic Confession Article 14.

Knowledge of Good and Evil you shall not eat, for in the day that you eat of it you shall surely die."

Now then, when you compare Genesis 2:17 to the definition of the Westminster Confession there is something that might strike you as slightly odd. The Confession says that God was promising life to Adam, but in Genesis 2:17 it is a promise of death if he breaks this covenant.

How do you suppose that the Westminster Assembly arrived at this understanding? One way to reach this conclusion is to look at it from the opposite end of the spectrum. If breaking this covenant means death, then keeping this covenant means life. And if we go back to Genesis 2:9 we do have a reference to the Tree of Life. Did Adam know about the Tree of Life? Evidently he did because when he was expelled from the garden, God stationed the cherubim at the entrance of the garden to keep Adam from returning and eating from the Tree of Life (Gen. 3:22).

The Westminster Confession of Faith and the Belgic Confession are highlighting the positive reward that is implicit in Genesis 2. There is a reward for Adam if he will do what God commands. This shouldn't come as a surprise since it is a theme found in many places in the Bible:

> [1]And if you faithfully obey the voice of the LORD your God, being careful to do all his commandments that I command you today, the LORD your God will set you high above all the nations of the earth. [2] And all these blessings shall come upon you and overtake you, if you obey the voice of the LORD your God. (Deut. 28:1-2)

> You shall therefore keep my statutes and my rules; if a person does them, he shall live by them: I am the Lord. (Lev. 18:5)

Speaking of the law, David writes, "Moreover, by them is your servant warned; *in keeping them there is great reward*" (Ps. 19:11; 58:11). The rich young ruler asked Jesus, "Teacher, what good deed must I do to have eternal life?" And he said to him, "Why do you ask me about what is good? There is only one who is good. *If you would enter life, keep the commandments*" (Matt. 19:16-17; emphasis mine). So also Paul, "For Moses writes about the righteousness that is based on the law, that *the person who does the commandments shall live by them*" (Rom. 10:5).

When we consider the covenant made with Adam in Genesis 2:17, there is something greater in store for Adam if only he would remain faithful to God by keeping the commandment. Adam was a living being (Gen. 2:7), but there was a greater kind of life that he had yet to experience. Strictly speaking, the reward wasn't life, because Adam already had life and death was only introduced when he sinned. His reward wasn't to receive a relationship with God, because he already had that too. His reward was not simply to have a great marriage and well behaved, sinless kids, to which parents say, "GLORY!" The life promised to Adam was something greater than the life he possessed before the fall. The older theologians called it eternal life. It would have been an eternal, unchangeable life.

We need to analyze some of the features and potential outcomes for Adam and the human race in the covenant of works. We will consider what the storyline would have looked like had Adam passed the test. Once we have done that, we will take up the fall and the covenant of grace.

I am going to lay out six points for the covenant of works, but before we get to them, I need to put my presupposition on the table. I am assuming that when Adam sinned, God did not scrap the destiny that he had offered to Adam in the covenant of works. Jesus takes believers to the very place that Adam could have gone. The reward that the Last Adam (Rom. 5:12ff., 1 Cor. 15:45) earns for his people is not something less than the wages the First Adam would have earned for himself and his descendants after him. *The destiny is the same; what changes is the way in which Adam and his elect offspring get there.* By reading the Bible this way, we can carefully use later scriptural passages as lenses to help us see more clearly the eschatology (the heavenly goal) of Genesis 1-3.

Having stated this presupposition, here are the six points that take us from Adam's origin to Adam's destiny by way of the covenant of works.

1. God created a sanctuary called the Garden of Eden. It was God's holy temple, and he put Adam in it.

2. God then entered into a covenant with Adam. Adam must not eat from the Tree of the Knowledge of Good and Evil.

3. If Adam would have continued in obedience, he would have been sealed in his righteousness and holiness, and there would not have been any chance that he or any of his descendants would have fallen into sin.

4. Adam and Eve would have gone on to have children, and gradually the whole earth would have been filled with God's holy, righteous image.

5. Adam and Eve and their growing family would have mirrored God in their work by subduing and cultivating the earth until it became one giant garden sanctuary.

6. At the end of this joyful work, God would consummate his creation, and the human race would experience glorification.

On this reading, there is a lot at stake, isn't there? One violation of the one command came with heavy consequences, but as we will see, God had a remedy that was ready and waiting. Let's go through the points.

1. God created a sanctuary called the Garden of Eden. It was God's holy temple, and he put Adam in it.
Why call the Garden of Eden a sanctuary or temple? You probably don't look at your garden as a sanctuary, and after gardening you probably don't look at the dirt under your fingernails as evidence of religious activities. Be that as it may, there are many good reasons for understanding the place of Adam's dwelling as an earthly shadow of a heavenly sanctuary.[3]

Solomon's temple was garden-like. In Genesis 2:8 we are told that God planted a garden. When Solomon built the temple, he used images that one would expect to find in a garden. The temple was adorned with gourds and open flowers (1 Ki. 6:18). The walls of the temple had engravings of palm trees and open flowers (6:29). The pillars of the temple had tworows of 200 pomegranates at the top of them (7:18-20). Solomon also set up ten lampstands before the inner sanctuary that resembled a small orchard of blossoming trees (7:49).[4]

Life-giving river. In Genesis 2:10-14 a river flows from Eden through the garden and spreads out in different directions to water the earth. Many years later, the prophet Ezekiel is given a vision of the future temple of God. He sees a river of water gushing from under the temple,

---

[3] For a massive sweep of biblical and extra-biblical evidence readers should consult Greg Beale's informative book, *The Temple and the Church's Mission,* New Studies in Biblical Theology (Downers Grove, IL: Intervarsity, 2004). Other fine treatments are G. J. Wenham, "Sanctuary Symbolism in the Garden of Eden Story," in *I Studied Inscriptions from Before the Flood:Ancient Near Eastern, Literary, and Linguistic Approaches to Genesis 1-11*, ed. R. S. Hess and D. T. Tsumura, Sources for Biblical and Theological Study 4 (Winona Lake: Eisenbrauns, 1994), 399-404. J.H. Walton in the IVP *Dictionary of the Old Testament: Pentateuch*, eds. T. Desmond Alexander and David W. Baker, (Downers Grove, IL: InterVarsity Press, 2003), 202-05. M. G. Kline, *Kingdom Prologue* (South Hamilton, MA: self published, 1993), 28-39.

[4] Beale, *Temple*, 72.

and from there it spreads out and waters the earth (Ezek. 47). When the temple's river reaches the sea, the water becomes fresh (47:9). Everything lives where this river goes. In the last book of the Bible, the final temple descends out of heaven having a river of the water of life flowing from the throne, and on the sides of the river is the Tree of Life (Rev. 22:1-3).

Cherubim. In Genesis 3:24, God stationed the cherubim to keep Adam out of the Garden of Eden. The entrance to the inner sanctuary of Solomon's temple is described as follows:

> For the entrance to the inner sanctuary he made doors of olivewood; the lintel and the doorposts were five-sided. He covered the two doors of olivewood with carvings of *cherubim, palm trees,* and *open flowers.* He overlaid them with gold and spread gold on the *cherubim* and on the palm trees. (1 Ki. 6:31-32; emphasis mine).

It is hardly coincidental that the Garden of Eden is blocked by cherubim and on the door to the inner sanctuary of Israel's temple, one was confronted with the cherubim amidst trees and open flowers. Solomon was making a connection between the Garden of Eden and the Jerusalem temple. Fruit trees, flowers, life-giving rivers, and cherubim; these things are found in the temple of Solomon, the temples seen by the prophets, and the Garden of Eden, causing a number of scholars to conclude that the Garden of Eden is the first temple in the Bible. And, of course, when people built temples, they put the image of their god in that temple. What does God put in this first garden temple? He puts his image in it, Adam and Eve (Gen. 1:27).

Adam as priest. Now if the Garden of Eden has the feel of a temple, could it also be that Adam is the first priest? Look with me at Genesis 2:15. "The Lord God took the man and put him in the Garden of Eden to work it and keep it."

It is thought by a number of Old Testament scholars that the words *to work…* and *keep…*[5] have a double meaning. On the one hand they describe the work of farming and agriculture. And that makes sense if Adam is going to be placed in a garden. Greg Beale has shown that there is a religious usage of these words. When these two Hebrew words are found in the Bible, they either refer to Israelites serving God and keeping his word, or they describe the function of the priest who keeps and guards the tabernacle.

In Numbers 8:24-27, Moses outlines the duties of the priests:

---

[5] *'ābad* and *shāmar.*

> [24] This applies to the Levites: from twenty-five years old and upward they shall come to do duty in the service [25] of the tent of meeting. And from the age of fifty years they shall withdraw from the duty of the service and serve no more. They minister to their brothers in the tent of meeting by keeping guard, [26] but they shall do no service.[27] Thus shall you do to the Levites in assigning their duties."[6]

The older priests are to *keep guard* while the younger priests *serve* in God's tabernacle. The temple was to be kept holy to the Lord. We know that Adam's life was to be lived in worship and service to God, but what would Adam need to be on his guard about? That is answered in Genesis 3. The unholy serpent comes in to God's temple to tempt Adam and Eve.

2. God then entered into a covenant with Adam. Adam must not eat from the Tree of the Knowledge of Good and Evil.

In Genesis 2:17 the covenant of works is made with Adam. God commands Adam not to eat of the fruit of the Tree of the Knowledge of Good and Evil lest he die. From Genesis 2:17 onward, Adam is in this solemn, binding relationship with God. This brings us to our third point.

3. If Adam would have passed the test, he would have been sealed in his righteousness and holiness, and there would not have been any chance that he or any of his descendants would have fallen into sin.

When God entered into this covenant with Adam, Adam had the ability to sin and not to sin. If he would have passed the test, he would have been sealed in his original righteousness and holiness and would not have been able to sin. This was not the first of a battery of tests for Adam. He was given one test, concerning one tree, and had he obeyed, life without the possibility of death would have been his.

If you think about it, this is really the comfort of eternal life in the new heavens and earth. There is absolutely no possibility of pain, sickness, suffering, and death in the eternal state. We do not receive a happy, sinless existence that can be lost. If that was the case, I would most certainly lose it! When Jesus passed the test for his people, we are guaranteed that in the life to come we will not be susceptible to sin and the curse. So also for Adam; he would have gone from being able to sin, to being unable to sin. And from this point onward, the blessings of the covenant would have been secured.

4. Adam and Eve would have gone on to have children, and gradually the whole earth would have been filled with God's holy, righteous image.

---

[6] Cf. Num. 3:7-8; 18:5-6; 2 Ki. 12:9; 1 Chr. 23:32; Ezek. 44:14.

5. Adam and Eve and their growing family would have mirrored God in their work by subduing and cultivating the earth until it became one giant garden sanctuary.

Points four through five really go together. Adam and Eve are not designed to live alone. They were not created to just stay in one little spot on planet earth. Genesis 1:28 makes that clear:

> And God blessed them. And God said to them, "Be fruitful and multiply and fill the earth and subdue it, and have dominion over the fish of the sea and over the birds of the heavens and over every living thing that moves on the earth.

We shouldn't assume that had Adam passed the test, he would have gone straight to heaven. There is a world that must first be filled with God's image and that glorious work was assigned to Adam and Eve. If Adam would have been immediately glorified, he would not have been able to populate the earth. When the Sadducees asked Jesus the question about the woman who had all of those husbands, "whose wife would she be in the age to come?" Jesus said to them that in that eternal age of glory, there will be no marrying for we will be like the angels (Matt. 22:30). This means that filling the earth must come first before final glorification. The Genesis 1 purpose of marrying serves a greater end and a greater joy than the union of husband and wife. The purpose of marriage is for the spread of the image of God. That is why it is given.

6. At the end of this joyful work, God would consummate his creation, and the human race would experience glorification.

As wonderful as life would have been on earth, there was something far better for Adam and his descendants than the lives they were living. Adam and all of his descendants would have enjoyed a greater life, a life that Paul describes as a glorified existence in a glorified body.[7]

Paul talks about these glorified bodies in 1 Corinthians 15. It is very important that we see the particular point of comparison that he is making between Adam and Christ. He is not comparing Adam the sinner with Jesus the righteous. He does make that contrast in Romans 5, but that is not the point of comparison in 1 Corinthians 15. Paul is comparing Adam before the fall with Jesus after the resurrection. The immortal, spiritual body is what we have to look forward to as sinners, and it was also what Adam had to look forward to had he remained sinless:

> It is sown a natural body; it is raised a spiritual body. If there is a natural body, there is also a spiritual body. (1 Cor. 15:44)

---

[7] Here I am following Greg Beale, *A New Testament Biblical Theology* (Grand Rapids: Baker, 2011), 43-45.

Now you might think that the natural body is the sinful body. But God did not give Adam a natural body that was sinful. Death is unnatural. His natural body became sinful. Notice the citation in the next verse:

> [45] Thus it is written, "The first man Adam became a living being"; the last Adam became a life-giving spirit. [46] But it is not the spiritual that is first but the natural, and then the spiritual. [47] The first man was from the earth, a man of dust; the second man is from heaven. (1 Cor. 15:45-47)

Paul is citing Genesis 2:7, not Genesis 3:19. Adam receives a natural body first. The life promised to Adam in the covenant of works was the reward of a spiritual body. On this reading, it is difficult to conclude that the spiritual body promised to us is something entirely different than the life that was promised to Adam. In 1 Corinthians 15, the contrast between Adam and Christ is the contrast between two sinless people. "The first man Adam" would have received a spiritual body that could never perish.

Summary

To put it plainly, there was a progression to an even greater glory for Adam. For keeping the covenant of works, he would have been kept free from future sin, suffering, sorrow, and death. He would have gone about his mandate to have children and take dominion of the earth with joy. When that work was completed, his natural body would have been transformed into a spiritual body. All of this was ahead for Adam.

Would there be any changes for the earth? There is at least one thing that the earth would have enjoyed after Adam and his descendants had finished filling it. The crowning reward of Adam and his children's work would be God himself descending to earth and dwelling among them. John describes this in Revelation 21:1-3:

> [1]Then I saw a new heaven and a new earth, for the first heaven and the first earth had passed away, and the sea was no more. [2]And I saw the holy city, new Jerusalem, coming down out of heaven from God, prepared as a bride adorned for her husband. [3] And I heard a loud voice from the throne saying, "Behold, the dwelling place of God is with man. He will dwell with them, and they will be his people, and God himself will be with them as their God.

The reward for Adam's obedience was the Lord coming down to earth to take up his eternal residence in the midst of his people in an unfallen world. In Revelation 21, John sees what will happen after the curse has been removed. Because sin has been atoned for and righteousness has been secured, God will dwell among his people face to face. Now, when we look at chapter 22, we find the River of Life and the Tree of Life in the new heavens and earth. And in v. 3 there is something even more spectacular:

> No longer will there be anything accursed, but the *throne of God* and of the Lamb will be in it, and his servants will worship him. (Emphasis mine)

Now a question, where is God's throne right now? In heaven. Where was God's throne when he created the earth? In heaven. The Garden of Eden, the tabernacle, and the temples of Israel were earthly copies of the heavenly temple (Heb. 8:5). And John sees the temple of God coming down, and God's throne will be upon the earth forever! That is the destiny and goal for Adam and his descendants in the covenant of works.

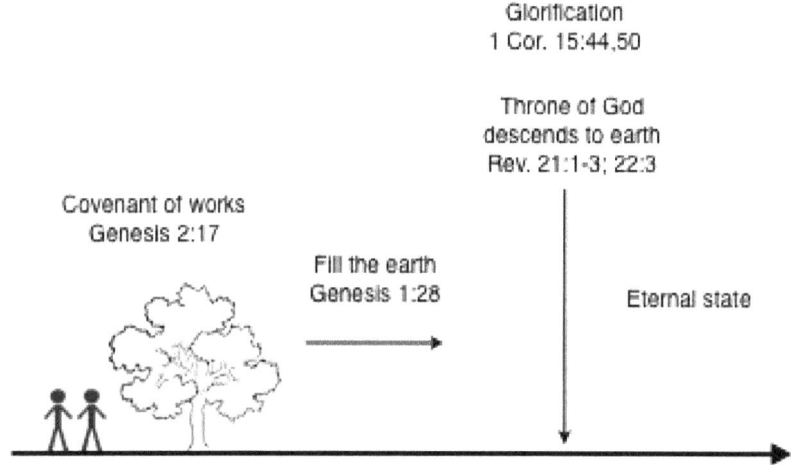

The Sovereign Lord sets the terms for the covenant of works, "do not eat the fruit of the Tree of the Knowledge of Good and Evil or you will die." The sovereign Lord offers the reward for obedience in the covenant of works. You will have great joy and pleasure filling the earth with people and making the earth a dwelling place for you and your family. When you are finished, I will give you a glorified body, and my throne will descend from heaven and be placed among you in a world-encompassing paradise completely walled off from any possibility of sin and curse. God did not spell all these things out for Adam in so many words,[8] but the seed is here in Genesis 2. The signs of the Sabbath rest, the garden sanctuary, and the Tree of Life are all signs to Adam of God's pledge to bring him into a greater enjoyment of a greater glory.

Even though Adam failed to get us there, God had already appointed a second Adam who would not only atone for our sins, but this second Adam will bring his elect people to the place where Adam would have brought the human race. Christ Jesus took upon himself the obligations of the covenant of works on behalf of his people and his time of testing was far more difficult and painful as it culminated in the cross.[9] And I remind you that everything in this covenant that God made with Adam was calculated for Adam's success. Satan had the more difficult job because Adam was created completely holy and righteous. He had an unfallen mind that knew the will of God, and he had an unfallen nature that could do the will of God. Adam was created in the image of God; he loved God and had fellowship with God. Tragically, in just one moment, he threw it all away:

> [1] Now the serpent was more crafty than any other beast of the field that the Lord God had made. He said to the woman, "Did God actually say, 'You shall not eat of any tree in the garden'?" [2]And the woman said to the serpent, "We may eat of the fruit of the trees in the garden, [3]but God said, 'You shall not eat of the fruit of the tree that is in the midst of the garden, neither shall you touch it, lest you die.'" [4]But the serpent said to the woman, "You will not surely die. [5]For God knows that when you eat of it your eyes will be opened, and you will be like God, knowing good and evil." [6]So when the woman saw that the tree was good for food, and that it was a delight to the eyes, and that the tree was to be desired to make one wise, she took of its fruit and ate, and she also gave some to her husband who was with her, and he ate. (Gen. 3:1-6)

---

[8] "We believe that God created man out of the dust of the earth, and made and formed him after His own image and likeness, good, righteous, and holy, capable in all things to will agreeably to the will of God. But being in honor, he understood it not, neither knew his excellency..." (Belgic Confession Article 14)

[9] What do you understand by the word "suffered"? That during his whole life on earth, but especially at the end, Christ sustained in body and soul the anger of God against the sin of the whole human race. This he did in order that, by his suffering as the only atoning sacrifice, he might set us free, body and soul, from eternal condemnation, and gain for us God's grace, righteousness, and eternal life. (Heidelberg Catechism Lord's Day 15, Q/A 37)

The serpent's subtlety

The earth had been formed (Gen. 1), the Garden of Eden prepared (Gen. 2), and upon creating man the Lord places him in his garden sanctuary and establishes his covenant with him (Gen. 2:15-17). It wouldn't take long for Adam's loyalty to the covenant to be tested. Moses tells us that the serpent is "more crafty." In what ways? Well there are several signs of his skill.

1. He goes to Eve not Adam, subtly usurping Adam's authority.

2. He comes twisting God's command with a question. "Did God say you can't eat from any trees?" As if he really cared. Oh Eve, word has just reached my ear. Is it true Eve? Is it true that God won't allow you to eat any of the fruit in this garden? What a pity to be under such a tyrant.

3. The serpent doesn't actually ever say, "Eat the fruit." He gets her to do what he wants without telling her to do it.[10]

4. Satan engages the woman by choosing his words carefully. In Genesis 2 there was a specific repetition of words:

V. 7 then the <u>Lord God</u> formed the man of dust from the ground...

V. 8 And the <u>Lord God</u> planted a garden in Eden...V. 9 And out of the ground <u>the Lord God</u> made to spring up every tree... V. 15 The <u>Lord God</u> took the man and put him in the garden... 16 And the <u>Lord God</u> commanded the man, V. 18 Then the <u>Lord God</u> said... V. 19 Now out of the ground the <u>Lord God</u> had formed every beast of the field... V. 21 So the <u>Lord God</u> caused a deep sleep to fall upon the man, V. 22 And the rib that the <u>Lord God</u> had taken from the man...[11]

When God revealed himself to Moses, he declared that he will be known by his covenant name, THE LORD (Ex. 6:2-4). When God enters into the covenant with Adam his covenant name is used; he is LORD. Now consider the dialogue between the woman and serpent in chapter 3:

> [1] ..."Did <u>God</u> actually say, 'You shall not eat of any tree in the garden'?" [2] And the woman said to the serpent, "We may eat of the fruit of the trees in the garden, [3] but <u>God</u> said, 'You shall not eat of the fruit of the tree that is in the midst of the garden, neither shall you touch it, lest you die.'" [4] But the serpent said to the woman, "You will not surely die. [5] For <u>God</u> knows that when you eat of it your eyes will be opened, and you will be like <u>God</u>, knowing good and evil." (Gen. 3:1b-5)

---

[10] I owe this observation to Dr. Iain Duguid who made this observation in a course on Biblical Hebrew at Westminster Seminary in California.

[11] Gordon Wenham, *Word Biblical Commentary, Vol. 1: Genesis 1-15* (Nashville: Thomas Nelson, 1987), 73.

The covenant name of God drops out and once they eat the fruit, it resumes, "And they heard the sound of the <u>Lord God</u> walking in the garden in the cool of the day..." (3:8). The covenant Lord is coming to pronounce judgment.

Adam's dying

The Lord said, "for in the day you eat of it you shall surely die" (Gen. 2:17). Though the dying process began slowly, the spiritual death happened immediately. Looking at Genesis 3 do you see any signs of spiritual death?

1. Adam and Eve can't stand the sight of each other. They try to cover up the image of God (3:7).

2. They hide from God (3:8).

3. Adam blames God and "the woman." *"The woman that you gave to me..."* Translation, "If you would not have given me this woman, we wouldn't be in this mess" (3:12).

4. Eve blames the serpent—she doesn't say, "I wanted to be like you, I wanted your authority and power." She does own that she was deceived but nothing is mentioned of her adding to God's commandment (3:3) or her desire to be in the place of God.

5. Gen. 3:24 suggests that given the opportunity, Adam would have attempted to steal from God.

One violation of one covenant obligation and Adam and the world are ruined. What's wrong with the world? Fortunately the answer was given in 2008:

> A psychologist found he could predict children's prospects by testing whether they could resist eating a marshmallow... The psychologist will be scanning their brains to find neurological roots of temptation. The "marshmallow test" one of the world's simplest and most successful behaviors experiments... proved conclusively that the longer a 4 year old child was able to wait before taking the marshmallow, the better were his or her chances of a happy and successful life. [12]

---

[12] *Sunday Times*, November 2, 2008.

The article goes on to argue that children who grabbed the marshmallow turned into teenagers who lacked self-esteem and experienced difficult relationships with peers. Those who waited turned out to be more socially competent, self-assertive, and academically successful.

I think a better answer to the problem of the world was given in another newspaper article many years ago. A newspaper invited several eminent authors to write essays on the theme, "What is Wrong with the World?" Here's how one author responded.

> Dear Sirs,
>
> I am.
>
> Sincerely yours,
>
> G. K. Chesterton

I have become the problem because Adam represented me when God made a covenant with him. I am guilty of Adam's offense. In Adam I sinned, and in Adam I died (Rom. 5; 1 Cor. 15:22). This is the reason why things go wrong in the world.

Adam and Eve have died spiritually. What have they lost? They have doomed themselves to death. They have doomed their children to the same fate. (They will learn how fragile their sad lives are going to be when Cain decides to kill his brother.) They cannot dwell in God's presence. The land is under a curse, and the goal of a glorified existence is shattered. That is a lot of damage! But here in Genesis 3, we are introduced to another covenant, the covenant of grace.[13]

The Lord said, "Because you have done this (speaking to the serpent), cursed are you above all livestock and above all beasts of the field; on your belly you shall go and dust you shall eat all the days of your life" (Gen. 3:14). This concept of licking the dust is just a way of saying that someone has been defeated. It means that they have been put down; that the foot has been placed upon the neck. But that is not quite what God says here. He does not say that the serpent will lick the dust. What does He say? He will eat it! The dust is the remains of Adam's decayed

---

[13] Doth God leave all mankind to perish in the estate of sin and misery? God doth not leave all men to perish in the estate of sin and misery, into which they fell by the breach of the first covenant, commonly called the covenant of works; but of his mere love and mercy delivereth his elect out of it, and bringeth them into an estate of salvation by the second covenant, commonly called the covenant of grace. (Westminster Larger Catechism Q/A 30)

body, "for you are dust, and to dust you shall return" (3:19). Even before the gospel is announced, Satan learned that though Adam and Eve have fallen into death, God was going to make him eat defeat. God would send the seed of the woman to crush the serpent's head. Adam would return to the dust, and the Lord would force the dust down Satan's throat. Satan was forced to ground on his belly; Adam would be raised from the dead on the last day.

Genesis 3:15 is the mother promise of the entire Bible. This is where we see the relationship between the covenant of grace and the covenant of works so clearly. In order for there to be a covenant of grace, Christ must undertake the covenant of works and perfectly obey his Father. He must come and bruise the head of the serpent and in turn experience the painful bruising of his heel. Both take place at the cross and the empty tomb.

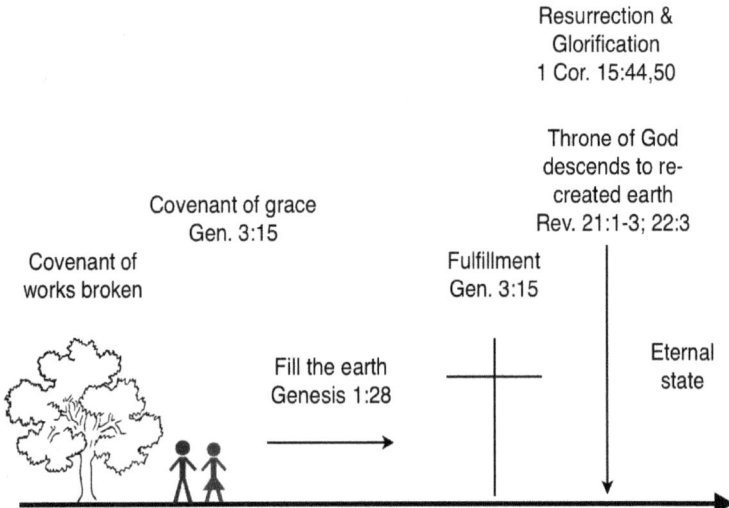

The initiative is entirely God's doing. Adam and Eve have sided with the devil. Here is why we believe in sovereign grace and election.[14] Note

---

[14] We believe that, all the posterity of Adam being thus fallen into perdition and ruin by the sin of our first parents, God then did manifest Himself such as He is; that is to say, merciful and just: merciful, since He delivers and preserves from this perdition all whom He in His eternal and unchangeable counsel of mere goodness has elected in Christ Jesus our Lord, without any respect to their works; just, in leaving others in the fall and perdition wherein they have involved themselves. (Belgic Confession, Article 16)

those words carefully, "I will put enmity between you and the woman." Classic Arminianism teaches that God regenerates people once they exercise their free will to believe. This passage paints a very different picture, showing that regeneration *precedes* faith. When the first need of salvation is revealed, a sovereign, irresistible grace is given. Regeneration and faith are not things that Adam, Eve, or anyone of us can produce. Salvation, right from the very beginning and all the way to the end, is entirely the work of God.

God tells the serpent that he will be judged and God will turn his peoples' hearts back to himself. Even though they have died spiritually and will die physically, he is guaranteeing the deliverer will come and defeat the prince of death. The question is, did Adam and Eve believe this promise? Did God regenerate them and give them faith to believe?

The biblical data points in this direction. "The man called his wife's name Eve, because she was the mother of all living" (Gen. 3:20). You would have thought that Adam, being ornery and cantankerous like he was just a few verses ago, would have named his wife "Death." He names her "Eve," which means "Life-giving." Now where did he get that idea? He got it by the promise of the gospel in verse 15. He understood that Eve was going to bring forth someone who would undo the mess that he had made. So he calls her "Life-giving." He heard the promise, and so he makes his declaration of faith.

The Gospel

Adam hears the condemnation of God, he has broken the law. He hears the judgment of God against his sin; he hears about the offspring of the woman who will defeat the serpent; he hears that God will turn his heart away from the serpent and to God, so he names his wife "Life" rather than "Death." And what does v. 21 go on to say? "And the Lord God made for Adam and for his wife garments of skins and clothed them." That sounds like the earliest form of the gospel to me. We hear God's law; we are convicted that we have broken it; we hear that God has sent Christ to defeat Satan; and God regenerates us. In turn we believe and cling to our Lord's gracious promises and are clothed with the righteousness of Christ.

Everything that we see unfolding in the Bible is subservient to the promises made in Genesis 3:15. That is why "offspring" is so important to the book of Genesis. In Genesis, Moses traces out where this offspring is coming from and to whom this offspring will be given. The New Testament shows us that this offspring is Jesus (Matt. 1:1)!

How does Jesus conquer? By living a holy and righteous life and resisting the temptations of the devil. No sooner is Jesus identified as the

Messiah, then he is driven into the wilderness to be tempted by the devil. Satan comes to him after his forty-day fast and tempts him to swerve from the path of obedience by turning a stone into bread. The wicked tempter comes to Jesus as he did to Eve, pretending to be a friend.

Jesus must have looked hungry. The serpent hissed, "If you are the Son of God, tell these stones to become bread" (Matt 4:2). This is no way for a father to treat his beloved son. Why not turn the stone into bread? You gave Israel manna in the wilderness, you need to care for yourself now and stop thinking about others. Jesus resists. and Satan comes at him again:

> "If you are the Son of God," he said, "throw yourself down. For it is written:
>
> "'He will command his angels concerning you,
>
> and they will lift you up in their hands,
>
> so that you will not strike your foot against a stone.'" (Matt. 4:6)

They say that you are the Messiah. The Anointed One, thought to be more powerful than all the prophets of old. Since the angels are charged with your care, why not jump off of the temple and let everyone know that the wait is over?

Once more the devil comes at him with a frontal attack. After showing him all the kingdoms of the world, he offers a proposal, "All this I will give you," he said, "if you will bow down and worship me" (v. 9). Let's not beat around the bush any longer. We both know that God has called you to a very difficult task. You are king. Kings have kingdoms, so I'll make you a deal. You can avoid all the pain and toil that your father, the king has for you. You need only bow down and worship me. You don't need to settle for being king of the Jews, I will give you all the nations of the world. All those nations promised to Abraham, I offer to you. Just one easy little act of worship, and all that sacrificial obedience can be avoided.

Jesus looks the worthless serpent in the face and said, "Away from me, Satan! For it is written, "'You shall worship the Lord your God and him only shall you serve'" (Matt. 4:10). "Him only shall you serve." It was a service that Jesus willingly underwent, living faithfully in covenant with God. There was a righteousness to perform and a payment to be made for the violation of the covenant. All was laid upon Jesus as he went to the cross to open the way to the Tree of Life.

There are two trees, the Tree of the Knowledge of Good and Evil and the Tree of Life. In 1 Peter 2:24 we find these words, "He himself bore our sins in his body on the tree,...." Why the tree? Why "tree" instead of cross? Peter reminds us that Christ overturned what Adam did. God forbids Adam and Eve to eat of a tree. God requires that Christ takes their place upon a tree. If I can paraphrase the words of A. W. Pink:[15] God commands Adam and Eve not to eat, but because of Christ we are commanded to eat of the fruits of Christ's labor upon the tree. Satan tries to get Adam to eat from the Tree of the Knowledge of Good and Evil and now he tries to prevent people from eating and drinking of the fruit of Christ's suffering upon the tree which is the way to eternal life in a glorified body, on a consummated new heavens and earth, with God's throne in his people's midst, forever.

Study Questions:

1. What was promised to Adam?
2. What reasons are given for viewing the Garden of Eden as an earthly temple?
3. What would have happened if Adam passed the test?
4. What is the relationship between the covenant of works and the covenant of grace?
5. Describe the gospel of Genesis 3.
6. How do these two covenants show us Christ?

---

[15] A. W. Pink, *Genesis* (Chicago: Moody; 1922), 27-32.

Chapter 3: The Covenant with Noah: Preserved for the Sake of Promise

> For they deliberately overlook this fact, that the heavens existed long ago, and the earth was formed out of water and through water by the word of God, and that by means of these the world that then existed was deluged with water and perished. But by the same word the heavens and earth that now exist are stored up for fire, being kept until the day of judgment and destruction of the ungodly. (2 Pet. 3:5-7).

> Forgetful heart, Lost your power of recall,
>
> Every little detail, You don't remember at all,
>
> The times we knew, Who would remember better than you,
>
> Forgetful heart, We laughed and had a good time, you and I,
>
> It's been so long, Now you're content to let the days go by..."
> (Bob Dylan)

Perhaps that was the mindset of man after the fall into sin. God has forgotten. The days will just roll on by as we live our own lives our own way. We have nothing to worry about. We are the masters of our own destinies. The world would soon learn that God does not forget. On the one hand that is wonderful news; God spoke words of rescue to Adam and Eve, and time did not dim his memory. Thank goodness he is not like us. He doesn't get busy with other projects and forget the world and the word of promise that he spoke to his people. That is great news! On the other hand it is also *bad* news. A holy God who remembers sin is a terrifying thing for those who know themselves to be sinners. God cannot forget the salvation that he promised to Adam and Eve, nor can he forget about sins committed against him. I suspect that is why the Bible so quickly turns to Noah. In the account of Noah, we see the severity of God's justice, the sweetness of God's grace, and the promise of his preservation of the world.

CHAPTER THREE

The covenant with Noah: What does it mean?

What is the covenant with Noah all about? We are accustomed to thinking of this covenant mainly in terms of the rainbow in the sky and God's promise not to cut off every living thing from the earth (Gen. 9:11). The covenant that God makes with Noah is his promise to preserve the earth. It is not a covenant about salvation so much as it is a covenant concerned with preservation. It has been called a covenant of common grace. The Lord also shows common grace to his entire creation by restraining sin and causing people to do that which is good (non-saving good) in the realm of society and family. The common grace element of the covenant with Noah is God's commitment to never again destroy the world with a flood (Gen. 8:21-22).[1] But why does he commit himself to this course?

How the covenant with Noah connects to the covenants of works and grace

God established the covenant with Noah for the sake of the covenant of grace (Gen. 3:15). An important point to remember is that the major covenants of the Bible are connected to one another. For the sake of his covenant of grace, God established the covenant of common grace. This covenant was put into place to preserve the world from the wrath of God being unleashed as in the flood. Because sin is found in every place and God is angry with sin every day (Ps. 7:11-12), the Lord covenants to stay his hand from destroying the world. The promised Messiah must come. He must enter the world, crush the serpent, liberate his people, and in the end bring them safely into the new heavens and earth to dwell with God forever.

The flood was a sign (2 Pet. 3:5-7). It was a forecast of a day that is coming when God will judge the world in righteousness. The Noahic covenant further unfolds how God will save his people by his grace (Gen. 6:8), through a righteous man of his choosing (Gen. 6:9; 7:1), who will do the will of God (Gen. 6:22), and so deliver his people (Gen. 7:7ff.) from the wrath of God (Gen. 6:13) and bring them into a new heavens and earth (Gen. 9). The covenant with Noah teaches us about our covenant-keeping Lord and Savior, Jesus Christ.[2]

---

[1] Other biblical examples of God's common grace can be found in Genesis 4:15, Matthew 5:45 and Romans 2:4.

[2] The question of whether or not we have one or two covenants here will not be discussed. Meredith Kline's argument for 2 covenants can be found in his book *Kingdom Prologue* (South Hamilton, MA: self

As we look at the context and details of the covenant made with Noah, I would like to draw your attention to six themes.
1. Sin is an offense against God.
2. God will judge sin in righteousness.
3. God will show grace to his people.
4. His grace will come through one who is righteous.
5. He will save his people from the wrath to come.
6. He will preserve the world until the day of his wrath.

Let's begin with the question, "Why was God angry?" Then we will look at the covenant with Noah.

The spread of sin

The darkness of sin began to spread rapidly after Adam and Eve's rebellion in the Garden of Eden. It was a growing problem that took root in the hearts of Adam and Eve as they stood next to the Tree of the Knowledge of Good and Evil. As we saw, because of their rebellion, Adam and Eve died to God and doomed the human race. They tried to cover up his image, they fled from his presence, and Adam blamed God and attempted to turn his wife out into the place of judgment. Grace was needed, and grace was given. God promised to put enmity between these rebels and the serpent. But as the story goes, it is not a grace that is given to all. The covenant of grace is for God to give to those he has chosen. The rest remain the offspring of the serpent, or as Jesus put it, "children of your father the devil" (Jn. 8:44). From this point onward until the end of the world, there are only two types of people, those who belong to the offspring of the woman and those who belong to the offspring of the serpent.

As it turned out, there would be lots of striking and deadly bruising in the history of the world. Not every child of Adam and Eve claimed God's gospel promise (Gen. 3:15). In Genesis 4, Cain contemplates murder. God warns him, but to no avail, and the ground underneath his feet was stained with blood. Like his father before him, Cain would not come clean and own up to his sin. God said, "Where is Abel your brother?" and Cain replied, "I DO NOT KNOW." He then sarcastically added, "Am I my brother's keeper?" So God pronounces a curse upon the murderer, and Cain's response was like so many we hear today. He was not sorry for what he did; he was sorry he got caught and punished (Gen. 4:13). His pride is astounding. He had no concern for his brother's life and thought nothing of taking it from him. When it comes to his own

---

published, 1993), 142-143. Probably the majority of interpreters understand there to be one covenant made with Noah.

life, then he worries (Gen. 4:14). By word and deed Cain showed himself to be an offspring of the serpent. Satan succeeded in masterminding the spiritual deaths of Adam and Eve. Cain succeeded in the physical death of his brother.

In his mercy, God gave Adam and Eve another son named Seth. The promises of God will not be buried in the ground with Abel but will continue through Seth all the way to the empty tomb of Jesus. It is through the line of Seth that the offspring of the woman will come. Yet tragically, widespread apostasy must come from this line first. Life under the curse goes on, but there is no evolutionary advancement making bad people better. Without the restraint of God, man is a savage. People do not get better over time like a good wine. Even the great majority of the line of Seth turned its back on the promises of God.

The problem: sin

> [2] The sons of God saw that the daughters of man were attractive. And they took as their wives any they chose. [3] Then the Lord said, "My Spirit shall not abide in man forever, for he is flesh: his days shall be 120 years." (Gen. 6:2-3)

The sons of God, or the line of the offspring of the woman, began to intermarry with the offspring of the serpent, the daughters of man.[3] The line separating the offspring of the woman and the offspring of the serpent had been crossed. The two lines had merged, and the tragic result of these marriage alliances is captured with a groan:

> [5] The Lord saw that the wickedness of man was great in the earth, and that every intention of the thoughts of his heart was only evil continually. [6] And the Lord was sorry that he had made man on the earth, and it grieved him to his heart. [7] So the

---

[3] There are three main interpretations of the *sons of God*. They are either Sethites, angels, or tyrannical kings from the line of Cain. The traditional interpretation of Sethites intermarrying with Canites seems most logical to my thinking. The immediate context is a genealogy (Gen 5:1-4). Adam is made in God's image and has a son (Seth) in his own image. Seth is a son of Adam, making Adam implicitly a son of God (a point Luke makes explicit, cf. Luke 3:38). The traditional interpretation also preserves the two offspring distinction unlike the angel interpretation. The third interpretation while plausible, does not explain how the actions of evil kings constitutes destruction of all people. However, if the Sethites are the sons of God intermingling with Canite women, it might go further to explain why God judges both lines. This is not to suggest that every Sethite man ended up marrying a Canite woman. It is probably a general description of the great majority rather than a small minority of Canite kings preying on the daughters of Seth.

> Lord said, "I will blot out man whom I have created from the face of the land, man and animals and creeping things and birds of the heavens, for I am sorry that I have made them." ⁸ But Noah found favor in the eyes of the Lord." (Gen. 6:5-8)

This is God's second universal assessment. In Genesis 1 the Lord steps back, as it were, and assesses what he has done: "...and the Lord saw that it was good." Chapter 1 concludes, "...and the Lord saw that it was very good" (Gen. 1:31). Chapter 6 is the painful contrast; "The Lord saw that the wickedness of man was great on the earth... now the earth was corrupt in God's sight" (Gen. 6:5, 11).

Every inclination of the human heart was bent upon evil. It was a self-seeking, evil-perpetrating mess. The wickedness that filled the human heart filled the earth with violence (v. 11). Cain killed his brother; Lamech kills man and child (Gen. 4:23); and the earth turns the sword on itself.

It is a disparaging assessment, as universal as the flood, *every*, *only* and *continually*. "Every intention of the thoughts of his heart." Everything their hearts longed for, every thought they lingered on, was only evil, *only evil*. Not sometimes their thoughts pleased God, and sometimes they didn't. It was every thought, only evil, continually. In vv. 11-13 we have the effect of the human heart upon the world:

> ¹¹ Now the earth was corrupt in God's sight, and the earth was filled with violence. ¹² And God saw the earth, and behold, it was corrupt, for all flesh had corrupted their way on the earth. ¹³ And God said to Noah, "I have determined to make an end of all flesh, for the earth is filled with violence through them. Behold, I will destroy them with the earth.

Three times in this passage Moses says that the world was corrupt and twice that the earth was filled with violence. *Corrupt* is not a bad translation, but it could also be translated *destroyed*. In v. 17 God declares that he is going to destroy the world. It is the same Hebrew word translated corrupt in vv. 11 and 12. It makes one wonder if it ought to read, "now the earth was <u>destroyed</u> in the sight of God and was filled with violence. And God saw the earth, and behold, it was <u>destroyed</u>, for all flesh had <u>destroyed</u> their way on the earth." Derek Kidner says "...what God determined to destroy, had been virtually self-destroyed."⁴

By way of application, the situation is no different today. God's assessment after the flood is the same as his assessment of the human condition before the flood, "...for the intention of man's heart is evil from his youth" (Gen. 8:21). Our hearts are riddled with sin that is eager

---

⁴ Derek Kidner, *Genesis* (Chicago: Intervarsity, 1967), 87.

to get out and express itself; it still desires to be master. Look at the world around you, and what do you find? Violence, greed, sexual immorality, and self-centeredness. These sinful vices are the disfigured hallmarks of every era. We do bad things because we make bad choices. We make bad choices because we have bad desires. And we have bad desires because we have a bad heart. Man is unable to do anything truly good so what must God do? He must carry out justice so that the guilty will be condemned, and he carries out his justice so that grace can be given. I put it that way because it isn't just a case of either justice or grace. God does not give grace at the expense of his justice. That is why both justice and grace are gifts most clearly demonstrated in the giving of the Son of God. He upheld the law of God, and he underwent the justice of God for our law-breaking, why? So that we would receive the grace of God and be given hearts that look only to Christ for a right standing before our righteous God. That is what we see happening in Genesis 6.

The solution: grace

The problem is sin, and the solution is declared, "I will blot out man whom I have created," but God's promise to Adam and Eve had not been forgotten. Noah was a member of the covenant of grace: "But Noah found favor in the eyes of the Lord" (Gen. 6:8). Noah was a recipient of God's *grace*. This is not the first time that *favor/grace* appears in the Bible, but it is the first time the word is used. Noah found favor/grace in the eyes of the Lord, and that's a great encouragement.

It means that in spite of the immeasurable corruption around us and within us, God's grace is greater. Noah found it. He did not earn it. It was not that Noah just happened to catch God's eye which led him to conclude that in those days nobody was perfect. Of course, he commits little sins; nevertheless, he couldn't possibly be condemned to hell for those trivial little infractions. Shall we call them mistakes? That is not how it worked. Noah found grace in God's sight. That means God had prepared it for him and applied it sovereignly to him. The world had gone bad, but God gives grace, and this is amazing grace.

Righteous and blameless

We have a wicked world, a gracious God, and in the third place we have a righteous Savior. Noah is the first man in the Bible who is described as *righteous* and *blameless*:

> These are the generations of Noah. Noah was a righteous man, blameless in his generation. Noah walked with God. (Gen. 6:9)

Clearly, Moses is using these words to contrast and compare Noah with the world. The world was corrupt; it was wicked, and it was filled with violence. By contrast, Noah was righteous and blameless, and the key is "in his generation." It is something like the apostle Paul's statement, "If anyone else thinks he has reason for confidence in the flesh, I have more: circumcised on the eighth day, of the people of Israel, of the tribe of Benjamin, a Hebrew of Hebrews; as to the law, a Pharisee; as to zeal, a persecutor of the church; as to righteousness under the law, blameless" (Phil. 3:4-6). Paul knew full well he wasn't blameless before God but when he is placed alongside of his contemporaries, he is, comparatively speaking, without fault. Though the world had walked away from God, there was still one who walked with God. As Noah stands before God, his righteousness and blamelessness are only by the imputation of Christ's righteousness, which is received by faith alone. Another way of saying it is, "and Noah found grace in God's sight." That inward grace made an outward distinction between Noah and his contemporaries. The world was wicked; Noah was righteous.

Kingdom building

Noah believed and obeyed God's word (Heb. 11:7). Noah did all that God commanded him (Gen. 6:22; 7:5). Noah built the one thing that could save him, his family, and the animals. The construction of the ark is intriguing to study, and in some ways it is reminiscent of the construction of the tabernacle and temple. There are several things that help us to make a connection between the ark and the tabernacle/temple of Israel.

A. God gives detailed architectural plans to Noah for the building of the ark and to Moses for the building of the tabernacle (Ex. 26-27, see also Ezek. 40-48; Rev. 21).

B. Noah is told to cover the ark "inside and out" with pitch (Gen. 6:14). The only other place the phrase "inside and out" occurs is in construction of the ark of the covenant. It was to be "overlaid with gold inside and out" (Ex. 25:11; 37:2).

C. The dimensions of the ark are given in cubits of length, breadth, and height (Gen. 6:15). The same repetition is used of the tabernacle and temple (Ex. 25, 1 Ki. 6:2). Both the temple and the ark stood thirty cubits high.

D. The ark had three decks (Gen. 6:16). The temple and the tabernacle had three sections, and the temple also had three levels (1 Ki. 6:8).

E. There is a distinction between clean and unclean animals (Gen. 7:2, 8) and, of course, this is very important to the later sacrificial system.

F. In Genesis 8:13, Noah removes the covering from the ark. *Covering* is used elsewhere of the hide of the tabernacle.[5]

G. The summary statement of the building of the ark is: "Thus Noah did; according to all that God commanded him, so he did" (Gen. 6:22, NKJV). The summary statement for the building of the tabernacle is: "Thus Moses did; according to all that the LORD had commanded him, so he did" (Ex. 40:16 NKJV).

In the book of Exodus, you have a certain progression. The Egyptians were brutally mistreating the Israelites. Israel cried out to the Lord. The Lord sent Moses to rescue them. Moses, as a baby, was placed in a tiny ark which is the same Greek word used only to describe Noah's ark. Moses delivered Israel. They passed through the sea, but their Egyptian enemies were drowned. Israel arrived at Mt. Sinai, and God entered into a covenant with his people. Then from chapter 25-31, you have Moses receiving instructions for making the tabernacle, after which sacrifices are made.

At the end of Seth's genealogy, Noah's father, the godly Lamech, cries out for relief because of their painful toil (Gen. 5:29), and the earth is filled with violence (Gen. 6:11). The Lord gives Noah the design to build the ark. Noah and his family pass through the waters while the enemies of God are drowned. God's covenant is given, and once Noah comes out into a new world, we find him on the mountain offering sacrifices to the Lord. The elements of tabernacle and temple building are anticipated in Genesis. Even the distinction between clean and unclean animals does not begin in Leviticus 11, but in Genesis 7.

Now when we stand back and survey the big picture, we begin to see more than just those cute little animals walking two by two into an ark prepared for them and Noah's family. We see in the constructing of the ark God's pattern for the redemption of his people. The ark is a small-scale picture of the kingdom of God.[6] In the ark the remnant are saved.

---

[5] Gordon Wenham, *Word Biblical Commentary, Vol. 1: Genesis 1-15* (Nashville: Thomas Nelson, 1987), 187. Cf. Ex. 26:14; 35:11; 36:19; 39:34; 40:19; Num. 3:25; 4:8, 10-12, 25.

[6] Kline, *Kingdom Prologue*, 140.

Noah did have a son who was not of God's elect, but that should not surprise us, for there will always be tares among the wheat until the eternal state arrives and purges out what never belonged (Matt. 13:30). The ark is the special place of God's saving presence. It is a pointer to a day when "the wolf and the lamb shall graze together; the lion shall eat straw like the ox" (Isa. 65:25).[7]

The place of salvation is rejected by the world

Not surprisingly, Noah is commended for his faith in God and his faithfulness in a twisted and corrupt generation. But remember that no one was commending him for building the ark in his day. Noah was a preacher of righteousness (2 Pet. 2:5), but the world covered its ears and refused to enter into the place that would protect them from the judgment.

Noah was no doubt mocked: "There goes crazy Noah again, out to cut down more trees so that he can continue building that giant box in his backyard. What a nut!" Do you suppose that Noah ever woke up, sore from the previous day's work, and thought to himself, "This is crazy, I am going back to bed?" Is it possible that when the construction wasn't going just right that Noah could have been tempted to turn the boat into firewood?

Noah was likely condemned by his culture as a lunatic, but he was commended by God for his faith, and it was a persistent faith. What kept him going? Obviously it was grace. And what did God use to communicate his grace? He used the covenant. "But I will establish my covenant with you, and you shall come into the ark, you, your sons, your wife and your sons' wives with you" (Gen. 6:18).

For decades Noah clung to God's covenant promise. What was it that God promised him? God promised that he would spare Noah and all who were with him and then destroy the world. Because Noah was a member of the covenant of grace, a member of the line of Seth that would lead to the Lord Jesus, God spared him so that his redemptive purposes could continue on in this fallen world. After decades of construction, the ark was completed:

> [1] Then the Lord said to Noah, "Go into the ark, you and all your household, for I have seen that you are righteous before me in this generation. [4] For in seven days I will send rain on the earth forty days and forty nights, and every living thing that I have made I will blot out from the face of the ground." (Gen. 7:1, 4)

---

[7] Correspondingly, in the ark the animals dwelt together peacefully.

Once again Noah's righteousness is highlighted. Why did God tell Noah to go into the ark? The answer is Noah was righteous. God said, "Go into the ark *for* I have seen that you are righteous before me in this generation" (emphasis mine). Again, this is not a righteousness by which Noah could stand before God on the last day and say, "something in my hands I bring," but it is a righteousness that was demonstrated by his commitment to the Lord to build the ark as God commanded him.

Upon completion of his service to Yahweh, the servant is welcomed into the ark and for seven days people woke up, they got dressed, ate their meals, tended their livestock, talked with friends, and celebrated life. Still no sign of a flood or Noah… still in the ark. On the seventh day the sky grew dark, and the earth began to convulse as the rain fell from above and the fountains of the great deep burst below (Gen. 7:11). "And the water prevailed" (Gen. 7:17). The fate of those who thought they could weather any storm is sealed in solemn repetition:

> [21] And all flesh died that moved on the earth, birds, livestock, beasts, all swarming creatures that swarm on the earth, and all mankind. [22] Everything on the dry land in whose nostrils was the breath of life died. [23] He blotted out every living thing that was on the face of the ground, man and animals and creeping things and birds of the heavens. They were blotted out from the earth. Only Noah was left, and those who were with him in the ark." (Gen. 7:21-23)

The earth is reduced to being formless and void all over again. In Genesis 1 we have creation; Genesis 7 is de-creation, a reversal of the created order. On day two of the creation week, God spoke the word, and the giant watery globe was separated into two parts. He created the expanse to separate the water from above and the water from beneath. Here in Genesis 7 the expanse is erased. God opened the windows of heaven, and the water came crashing back together. On day 3 of the creation week, the waters were pulled back and set in their place so that the land could appear. In Genesis 7 God released the water upon the earth and the land disappeared. The order of life was land, birds, livestock, creeping things, beasts and man (1:21-27). The order of death and de-creation was land, birds, livestock, beasts, swarming creatures, and man (7:20-21). It is here that we are confronted with the horrific nature of Adam's sin. "The flood is only the final stage in a process of cosmic disintegration that began in Eden."[8] This is what the violation of

---

[8] D. J. A. Klines, cited in Paul R. Williamson, *Sealed with an Oath*, New Studies in Biblical Theology (Downers Grove: Apollos/IVP; 2007), 60.

the covenant of works brought the world. It meant the undoing of the world.

God is just, and the world perished. God is also gracious, and eight souls were spared. God's covenant was established with Noah (Gen. 6:18) and Noah and his family were saved. God keeps his covenant promises. Inside the ark was a righteous man and his family, outside the ark were the masses of people drowned in the waters of God's judgment. God did not forget the covenant he had made, and he did not forget the righteous man he made it with. The way in which Moses captures God's remembering is striking.

"In 7 days I will send rain" (7:4).
  "After 7 days the waters of the flood came" (7:10).
    "The flood continued 40 days" (7:17).
      "And the waters prevailed on the earth 150 days" (7:24).
  But God remembered Noah. (8:1).
      "At the end of 150 days the waters had abated" (8:3).
    "At the end of 40 days Noah opened the window" (8:6).
  "He waited another 7 days" (8:10).
"Then he waited another 7 days" (8:12).[9]

This numerical structuring of the flood points us to what lies at the center: "But God remembered Noah…" This is a common expression which basically means that when the Lord remembers, he acts.[10] God entered into a covenant with righteous Noah. Noah built the ark, and Noah and his family were saved. God is faithful to his covenant.

This amazing deliverance of God's people is the first of many in the Bible. Most notably, the deliverance of the children of Israel from Egypt is anticipated in Noah's escape from the mighty floods of death. As Sailhamer has observed:

> The description of God's rescue of Noah foreshadows God's deliverance of Israel in the Exodus. Just as God "remembered

---

[9] This literary feature is called a chiasmus. Cf. Wenham, *Genesis, Vol. 1*, 156-157.

[10] Wenham, *Genesis, Vol. 1*, 184. God remembered Abraham and spared Lot (Gen. 19:29) he remembered Rachel (Gen. 30:20) and Hannah (1 Sam. 1:19) and gave them children. Because the Lord remembered his covenant with the patriarchs Israel would be brought out of slavery (Ex. 2:24; 6:5).

his covenant" (Ex 2:24) and sent "a strong east wind to dry up the waters before his people" (Ex 14:21) so that they "went through the dry ground" (Ex 14:21-22), so also in the story of the Flood we read that God "remembered" those in the ark (8:1) and sent a "wind" (8:1) over the waters so that his people might come out on "dry ground" (8:13-14).[11]

In both cases the Lord saves because of his commitment to keep the covenant he has made. We can never be more secure than in a relationship with a God who never fails to keep his word. As you read this, take heart; the sovereign Lord who brought Noah through the flood and Israel through the Red Sea is your covenant-making and covenant-keeping father who set his love on you before time began, covenanting with the Son and the Spirit to save you. If God is for you, who can stand against you (Rom. 8:31)?

Re-creation

With the old world destroyed, a new world emerges. In Genesis 1:2 the earth was covered in watery darkness, but the Spirit of God was hovering over the waters. That word *Spirit* is the Hebrew, *rûaḥ*. In Genesis 8:1 God made a wind (*rûaḥ*) blow over the earth, and the waters subsided. The *rûaḥ* was over the water at the creation week, and the creation was called forth. The *rûaḥ* blew over the watery earth, and the world reappeared. The earth was, once again, made habitable by the subsiding and separation of water so that the land could reappear.

Living creatures were brought out to populate the earth reminding us of days four through six of the creation week. In Genesis 1, days and seasons were established, and in Genesis 8:22, days and seasons were again fixed. Adam and Eve were told to be fruitful and multiply, and Noah and his sons were likewise commissioned (9:1, 7). As Adam and Eve were given dominion over the animals, so also was the dominion mandate reassigned to Noah and his family (vv. 2-4).

Of course the one significant difference is that Noah and his family went into a new world with an old problem. Noah still knew himself to be a sinner. He came out of the ark understanding what human nature was capable of doing and what God could very well do again in response. Out of his recognition of his insufficiency and need, he offered sacrifices. This was the only way he could approach a holy God. Noah's sacrifice showed that he still must approach God through the shedding of blood. It was a recognition that if he would live in God's world, it will

---

[11] John Sailhamer, *The Meaning of the Pentateuch* (Downers Grove: Intervarsity; 2009), 127.

have to be on the basis of God's mercy. So Noah offered a burnt offering sacrifice in 8:20.

Noah needed reassurances in this new world because he had no assurances that he and his descendants would be able to do anything less than call down the wrath of God by their sins. So the Lord repeated the promise again and again to Noah. He will never destroy the world with a flood. God bound himself with a covenant to stay his hand.

As a further assurance of his promise, the Lord stooped down from heaven and placed a sign in the sky. After getting a first-hand look at the ugliness of sin, God gave Noah a beautiful rainbow as a pledge that the earth would not be obliterated by the waters above and beneath. Who is the sign for? It was for Noah and for us, but only in a secondary way. In Genesis 9:16 God told Noah why he gave him the sign of the rainbow. "When the bow is in the clouds, I will see it and remember the everlasting covenant between God and every living creature of all flesh that is on the earth."

God puts the rainbow in the sky so that he will see it and remember. I suspect that would be very encouraging to Noah because that is how it began. When God created the world, the refrain went "and God *saw* that it was good" (emphasis mine). But in the days of Noah God *saw* that the earth had become corrupt and man had corrupted his way (6:12). In this new world, God *sees* the sign of his covenant, and he refrains from submerging the world under water. Walter Brueggemann writes, "The bow at rest thus forms the parallel to the Sabbath rest in 2:1-4 at the resolve of creation. The first creation ends with the serene rest of God. The re-creation ends with God resting his weapon."[12] The world is protected from God's wrath.

Noah comes out of the ark, and in ways reminiscent of Adam's fall in the Garden of Eden, Noah sins. Noah goes into a new world and plants a vineyard. He drinks himself drunk. He sins by the fruit of the vine, and he is found naked. His son also sins against him, and a curse is pronounced. Like Cain, who went off to build a city after the name of his son, so the nations descending from Noah's sons are city builders seeking to make a name for themselves. The need for the promise of Genesis 3:15 was just as great. Sin stains the new world, and one can imagine that after this chain of sinful events there could very easily be a sense of dread and fear when the clouds came heavy with rain. But God's covenant people, despite their sins, were reminded by the sign of the

---

[12] W. Brueggemann, *Genesis* (Atlanta: Westminster John Knox Press, 1982), 84-85.

covenant in the sky that God would remember and refrain from sending another world-wide flood.

It was because of mankind's sin and because of God's promises to do something about his people's plight that the world is preserved. Redemption will be accomplished by one who is greater than Noah.

The covenant of common grace and the coming of Christ

Through the life of Noah, God's people are given a clearer picture of what the promised offspring (Gen. 3:15) would be like as well as what he would do. What we have learned is that God will establish his covenant with a righteous man. Righteous and blameless Noah is instructed to build an ark. The ark is the place of salvation which bears striking similarities to Israel's tabernacle and temple. The ark is the place where the people in covenant with God are gathered. It is the one thing that will pass through God's judgment when it is poured out upon the earth. The earth is turned back to a globe of water, but God remembered his covenant with his servant. The *rûaḥ* of God blows over the waters and the seas return to their place. Dry land appears, and all who are inside the ark come out into a new earth. Noah offers sacrifices to God, and God blesses his people and gives the sign of his covenant commitment to never again bring the mighty waters to cover the earth.

The details of Adam and Eve's promised offspring are expanded in God's covenant partner, Noah, who was himself a type of Jesus Christ, the second Adam (1 Cor. 15:45). God showed mercy because of one man's faithfulness. Doesn't that sound familiar to you? The light of God's glory and grace shining upon Noah casts the shadow of Christ.

God establishes his covenant with his eternal Son who is truly righteous and blameless. Noah was a preacher of righteousness (2 Pet. 2:5). Jesus came preaching the kingdom of God and calling upon people to enter by faith in him. Noah was faithful and built the ark. He did all that God commanded him. Noah's obedience is eclipsed by the obedience of Jesus, who wasn't just obedient in life, he was obedient unto death, even death on a cross (Phil. 2:8). He could look at all the work given to him by his father to perform and say, "It is finished" (Jn. 19:30). Noah was remembered in the ark, but Jesus was forsaken upon the cross (Ps. 22:1; Mk. 15:34). All things outside the wooden ark died, but Jesus died upon the wooden cross, the covenant mediator, cut off for the sins of his people. Jesus is greater still. Noah left the empty ark and brought his family with him; Jesus exited the empty tomb securing his family's resurrection. We have been raised with him (Rom. 6:1-5; Col. 3:1-3).

It took years for Noah to build the ark, an ark that theologically resembled the tabernacle and temple. From the first gospel promise in the Garden of Eden, Jesus has been building the temple of God, the place where his name will be forever, the church:

> [19] So then you are no longer strangers and aliens, but you are fellow citizens with the saints and members of the household of God, [20] built on the foundation of the apostles and prophets, Christ Jesus himself being the cornerstone, [21] in whom the whole structure, being joined together, grows into a holy temple in the Lord. [22] In him you also are being built together into a dwelling place for God by the Spirit. (Eph. 2:19-22; cf. 1 Cor. 3:16-17; 6:19; 2 Cor. 6:16; 2 Thess. 2:4).

The *rûaḥ* blew upon the waters that brought death, the *rûaḥ* of God blows where it wills, and people, born of water and Spirit, live (Jn. 3:5-8). Noah and his family entered into a new earth, and Noah offered sacrifices to God. Jesus offered himself as a sacrifice (Heb. 7:26-28) to bring us into the new heavens and earth (2 Pet. 3:13; Rev. 21-22). Noah and his family are given a covenant sign of God's common grace. It was a sign that reminded them that God would not cut the world off with a flood. Christ's church is given a covenant sign of saving grace to remember that Jesus was cut off for the complete forgiveness of all our sins. "Do this in remembrance of me," said Jesus (Lk. 22:19). Noah entered a new world still riddled with sin but preserved by God's common grace. Christ will bring his people safely to a new earth where sin and curse are no more (Rev. 22:3); a place where sin and curse can never return (Isa. 25:8; 32:17-18; Rev. 22:14-15) because of Adam and Noah's redeemer, Jesus Christ our Lord.

The story of redemption is that God does not deliver except by a deliverer. Noah goes out of the ark and falls into sin. Moses leads the nation of Israel out of Egypt, but Moses will disobey (Num. 20:8, 11-12). Sampson repeatedly triumphs over the Philistines and was himself conquered by lustful rebellion. The nation of Israel forsook the Lord and was pursued with famine and with the sword until they were taken captive into exile. Before the exile overtook them, the voice of a prophet cried out with words of assurance:

> [9] This is like the days of Noah to me: as I swore that the waters of Noah should no more go over the earth, so I have sworn that I will not be angry with you, and will not rebuke you. [10] For the mountains may depart and the hills be removed, but my steadfast love shall not depart from you, and my covenant of peace shall not be removed," says the Lord, who has compassion on you. (Isa. 54:9-10)

For the sake of his previous promise (Gen. 3:15), God made a covenant with Noah and the world, a covenant of common grace, promising to hold his own sovereign hand back from plunging the world into destruction. Through the life of righteous and blameless Noah, God revealed the character of his son, promised to Adam and Eve. In order for Adam and Eve to escape God's wrath, the Son of God had to go to the place of no escape and offer up himself as a sacrifice upon the cross. And because of that wooden cross, his people will rejoice as they follow the Lamb of God, who leads them into a new world free from sin and curse. For thousands of years the people of God waited and watched until the day arrived when God himself stepped into the gap that had been widened by human sin and transgression and fulfilled the righteous demands of the covenant of works so that we could be the benefactors of the covenant of grace:

> His oath, his covenant, his blood
> Support me in the whelming flood;
> When all around my soul gives way,
> He then is all my hope and stay.
> On Christ, the solid Rock, I stand;
> All other ground is sinking sand,
> All other ground is sinking sand.[13]

Study Questions:

1. Why did God make a covenant with Noah?
2. What were some of the problems in Noah's day?
3. Why is *offspring* significant?
4. How is it that Noah can be called righteous and blameless?
5. How does Noah's ark resemble Israel's temple?
6. What points of contact are there between the account of the flood and Genesis 1?
7. What does God *remember* in this covenant?
8. What role does the Noahic covenant have in the covenant of grace?
9. How does the Noahic covenant point us to Christ?

---

[13] Edward Mote, "My Hope is Built" (1863).

Chapter 4: The Abrahamic Covenant: A Place for Abraham's People

> [1] Now the Lord said to Abram, "Go from your country and your kindred and your father's house to the land that I will show you. [2] And I will make of you a great nation, and I will bless you and make your name great, so that you will be a blessing. [3] I will bless those who bless you, and him who dishonors you I will curse, and in you all the families of the earth shall be blessed." (Gen. 12:1-3)

O. Palmer Robertson gives us the following survey of Abraham's life:

> God had promised to Abraham a land flowing with milk and honey, yet he possessed not one single inch of the designated territory. God had promised that he would be a blessing to all the nations, but plagues came upon the Egyptians because of Abraham's deceitfulness. All the wombs of the household of Abimelech were shut up because of Sarah, Abraham's wife. Is that what should be called being a blessing to the nations? God had promised Abraham that his offspring would be as numerous as the sand of the seashore, yet he had not one single child to claim as his own.[1]

How the Abrahamic covenant connects to the previous covenants

God's promises are going to advance through this most unlikely individual in order that it might be seen that God is not relying on anyone or anything to help him fulfill the promises that he had made. In terms of covenant theology, we would say that the covenant made with Abraham, and all the major covenants between God and man afterward, are expansions of the Genesis 3:15 promise: " I will put enmity between you and the woman and between your offspring and her offspring, he shall bruise your head and you shall bruise his heel."

---

[1] O. Palmer Robertson, *Covenants: God's Way With His People* (Suwanee: Great Commission Publications, 2003), 41.

Now the million dollar question is, "Who is the offspring?" It wasn't Abel, because Cain killed him, and it certainly wasn't Cain, who carried on the deadly deeds of the serpent. It is through the line of Seth that the promised offspring would come. But by the time we get to Genesis 6, the two lines have all but merged (Gen. 6:2-3). The evil had escalated to such proportions that God took action and destroyed the world with a flood. Once again, God makes a covenant, this time with Noah, and this will be a point we return to when we talk about baptism; when God makes a covenant, he includes the family. Noah's family comes with him into the ark, even Ham, who is from the line of Seth, but ultimately shows himself to be an offspring of the serpent. Yet because God makes a covenant with Noah, even Ham receives the temporal blessings.

Incidentally, do you suppose that it might be significant that Noah has three sons? Adam and Eve had many sons and daughters, but only three are mentioned: Abel, Cain, and Seth. God destroyed the world in the flood and started over with Noah, who also had three sons: Shem, Ham, and Japeth. And when God starts over again, once again it comes back to three individuals: Abraham, Isaac, and Jacob. God is ordering history according to his own sovereign decree, and this unbreakable will of God shapes the world and the narrative of the Bible.[2]

Noah came out of the ark after the flood, and the command given to Adam was reissued, "be fruitful and multiply, fill the earth" (Gen. 9:1), but the human race degenerated and rallied around a tower they had built which they thought would reach the heavens. Instead, God scattered them throughout the earth (Gen. 11:1-9). Once again, God starts over with one man who will carry on the promises of the covenant of grace. God will make him fruitful and will multiply him (Gen. 17:6). The call of Abraham in Genesis 12 provides a clearer picture of the blessings of the covenant of grace.

---

[2] Gentry and Wellum offer a similar observation, "Here, after Adam and Noah, God is making another new start. Abram and his family constitute another Adam. Notice the parallels in the biblical narrative: Adam and Eve had three sons (besides other children who are not named in the text; Gen. 5:4). Similarly, the genealogy in Genesis 5 ends with a man who also had three sons (Shem, Ham, Japheth). The genealogy in Genesis 11 ends in the same way: with a man who had three sons (Abram, Nahor, and Haran). This parallel is a literary technique inviting the reader to compare Abram with Noah and Adam." Peter J. Gentry and Stephen J. Wellum, *Kingdom Through Covenant: A Biblical Theological Understanding of the Covenants* (Wheaton: Crossway, 2012), 224.

Blessings through Abraham

> ¹ Now the Lord said to Abram, "Go from your country and your kindred and your father's house to the land that I will show you. ² And I will make of you a great nation, and I will bless you and make your name great, so that you will be a blessing. ³ I will bless those who bless you, and him who dishonors you I will curse, and in you all the families of the earth shall be blessed." (Gen. 12:1-3)

What is most striking about these verses is the primacy of the Hebrew word for blessing.[3] It occurs five times. That repetition is not accidental. In the first eleven chapters of Genesis, the curse is mentioned five times.[4] God curses the serpent, the earth, Cain, the earth (mentioned as cursed), and finally Canaan (3:14, 17; 4:11; 5:29; 9:25). The underlying message is clear. God is countering the curse with his power to bless. The end of v. 3 is particularly important as it is the goal of God's call to Abraham: "In you all the families of the earth shall be blessed."

Who are the families? Following the flow of Genesis, we should again take our cue from the context and conclude that the families are the nations that are scattered in the previous chapters:

> From these the coastland peoples spread in their lands, each with his own language, by their clans, in their nations. (Gen. 10:5)

If you have the English Standard Version, you might want to make a note that the word *clans* is the same Hebrew word translated *families* in Genesis 12:3. The following is from the New King James Version.

Genesis 10:18 The Arvadite, the Zemarite, and the Hamathite. Afterward the <u>families</u> of the Canaanites were dispersed.

Genesis 10:20 These *were* the sons of Ham, according to their <u>families</u>, according to their languages, in their lands *and* in their nations.

Genesis 10:31 These *were* the sons of Shem, according to their <u>families</u>, according to their languages, in their lands, according to their nations.

Genesis 10:32 These *were* the <u>families</u> of the sons of Noah, according to their generations, in their nations; and from these the nations were

---

[3] *bārak*.
[4] James McKeown, *Genesis*, The Two Horizons Old Testament Commentary (Grand Rapids/Cambridge: Eerdmans, 2008), 74.

CHAPTER FOUR

divided on the earth after the flood.

All of these guilty families lead up to the apostasy at the tower of Babel. All the families of Noah went astray. But when God calls Abraham, he says in essence, I am going after them. In you, Abraham, all the families of the earth shall be blessed. The five-fold blessing of chapter 12 answers the dilemma of the families mentioned five times in chapter 10. Even the Canaanites aren't completely cut out of God's covenant promises because Judah will go on to marry a Canaanite (Gen. 38). Amazingly, there is cursed Canaanite blood in Jesus' blood line!

Though all mankind went astray and each one turned their own separate way, God was not going to allow them to stay in darkness. The plan of the covenant of redemption and the covenant of grace is not just to have a specific race of people living in a specific place in the Middle East. The plan all along was a global plan. It was a plan that would bring about enmity between the devil and God's elect people by the striking of the offspring's heel (Gen. 3:15). This offspring will be a righteous and blameless Son (Gen. 6:9) who will do all that God commands (Gen. 6:22) and will save all his family (Gen. 8:18). This plan, for this particular offspring, was coming through Abraham's family. Abraham was chosen by God to be the means by which God's covenant grace would be brought to the nations.

The Abrahamic covenant is a covenant of grace which has as its goal the salvation of God's elect people, in the nations of darkness. I am not talking about a Christianizing of the world, but I am saying that nothing less than every tribe, tongue, and people will find themselves claimed by God's grace as he now expands to global proportions the promise he made to Adam and Eve in the garden.

In this sense Abraham stands in our Bibles as an Adam-like figure. In Genesis 2 Adam is formed outside of the Garden of Eden. God then brings him into the Garden and enters into a covenant with Adam. We find a similar situation with Abraham. Abraham receives his call in Ur of the Chaldeans (Mesopotamia). He is to go to the land described in Genesis 13:10 as the Garden of the Lord, and in that land God makes a covenant with him.

There is one more rather striking correspondence between Adam and Abraham. In both Genesis 3 and in the incident with Hagar in Genesis 16, the woman takes the lead.[5] Both wives give something to their husbands. The sequence is identical in both passages. Eve took the fruit,

---

[5] John Sailhamer, *The Meaning of the Pentateuch* (Downers Grove: Intervarsity; 2009), 154.

and gave it to her husband (Gen. 3:6). Sarai, Abram's wife, took Hagar… and gave her to her husband (Gen. 16:3). In Adam's case he rejects the terms of the covenant by eating the fruit of the Tree of the Knowledge of Good and Evil. In Abraham's case he stumbles over the promises of the covenant to have a son and takes another woman to achieve that purpose.

Adam fails and Abraham fails, but then again the promise does not depend upon these fathers but upon a certain Son who is the offspring of the woman.

The Abrahamic covenant: offspring and land

"Father Abraham, has many sons, many sons has Father Abraham…" Maybe you sang that in Sunday school when you were a child? I suspect if you would have sung it around Sarah she might have glared at you. The problem is that they didn't have any children. They had been living in the land for quite some time; they had been living on a promise that God was going to make their offspring great. But these promises of land and offspring are the very things that they do not have. They own no land, and they have no children:

> [1] After these things the word of the Lord came to Abram in a vision: "Fear not, Abram, I am your shield; your reward shall be very great." [2] But Abram said, "O Lord God, what will you give me, for I continue childless, and the heir of my house is Eliezer of Damascus?" [3] And Abram said, "Behold, you have given me no offspring, and a member of my household will be my heir." (Gen. 15:1-3)

If you look at v. 3 some translations say, "behold you have given me no offspring" others say "no seed." That word translated *seed* or *offspring* can be singular or plural. One day I walked downstairs, and my daughter came running up to me with a bowl of popcorn and said, "Look daddy, I have popcorns." Popcorn is a collective noun. Popcorn can be singular or plural, and the same is true with the word *offspring*.

In the case of Genesis 15, *offspring* is used in both the singular and the plural and that, I believe, deliberately so. The Lord is reshaping Abraham's thinking to get him to hope for more than the eye can see. When Abraham makes the statement in v. 3 "You have given me no offspring," what exactly is he asking God for? I think the answer is that Abraham is saying, "I would be very happy to have even one son." He is not asking for a lot, just one. This is confirmed at the end of v. 3 where Abraham says, "…and a member of my household will be my heir." Because Abraham has no biological offspring to give his wealth to, he will have to give it to his servant Eliezer. But God refuses to allow

Abraham to settle for a servant of his house. He states that one coming from Abraham's very own body will be his heir. Even after he impregnates his wife's servant, Hagar, God tells him that he will have a son through Sarah (Gen. 17:15). The Lord brings Abraham outside and shows him the stars and said, "So shall your offspring be" (Gen. 15:5). God promises Abraham one offspring (v. 4) and many offspring (v. 5). And Abraham not only understands it, but as v. 6 says, "...he believed the Lord, and he counted it to him as righteousness." Abraham takes God at his word, and God takes the righteousness of his son, that Son promised to Adam and Eve in the Garden of Eden, and applies his righteousness to Abraham. Abraham's justification is not based upon any sacrifice that he makes (Gen. 12:1, 4), any remorse he might feel (Gen. 13:4), or any heroic act he undertakes (Gen. 14). He stands in a right relationship with God, by faith. The Heidelberg Catechism asks, "How are you right with God?" and answers the question this way:

> Only by true faith in Jesus Christ. Even though my conscience accuses me of having grievously sinned against all God's commandments and of never having kept any of them, and even though I am still inclined toward all evil, nevertheless, without my deserving it at all, out of sheer grace, God grants and credits to me the perfect satisfaction, righteousness, and holiness of Christ, as if I had never sinned nor been a sinner, as if I had been as perfectly obedient as Christ was obedient for me. All I need to do is to accept this gift of God with a believing heart. (Heidelberg Catechism Lord's Day 23, Q/A 60)

Abraham cries out to the Lord in his inability and need. He is childless (Gen. 15:2-3). He was promised a reward (Gen. 15:1) but has no child of his own for it to be passed on to. How can he be a blessing to the world? How can he be made into a great nation when he doesn't even have a single child? And God swears that he will have one child and many children. It is the bare word of God, infused with sovereign, gracious power, and Abraham believes this promise. Though the promise goes against the facts of old age and bareness, despite the fact that there are no immediate signs that barren Sarah is about to conceive; nevertheless, Abraham believes God and is reckoned as righteous. All the merits of the Son of promise, Jesus, are applied to him.

God announces that he will give a single offspring (v. 3), through whom would come many offspring (v. 5), the promises of God are received by faith (v. 6), and the Promised Land is guaranteed as a possession (vv. 7, 18). The good news of the gospel of God's free grace is preached to Abraham on that day. And God's grace comes by way of the covenant:

> On that day the LORD made a covenant with Abram, saying, "To your offspring I give this land, from the river of Egypt to the great river, the river Euphrates." (Gen. 15:18)

The covenant of grace isn't just grace to get us through yet another day; it is grace that leads us home. It is grace bringing us to the goal, paradise in the presence of God. There was a garden land for Adam, a land like the Garden of the Lord for Abraham's descendants (Gen. 13:10), and there is a future land for the people of God that is described with garden-like imagery (Rev. 21-22). Those who believe in covenant theology are sometimes accused of spiritualizing Scripture. We do believe that the Promised Land was a physical land. But that land was a pledge of a better land. The writer of Hebrews tells us that Abraham was, "…looking forward to the city that has foundations, whose designer and builder is God" (Heb. 11:10).

The same thing is said of Israel. Even while Israel lived in the Promised Land, his saints knew that it was a pledge of a better country, a heavenly land:

> [13] These all died in faith, *not having received the things promised*, but having seen them and greeted them from afar, and having acknowledged that they were strangers and exiles on the earth. [14] *For people who speak thus make it clear that they are seeking a homeland.* [15] *If they had been thinking of that land from which they had gone out, they would have had opportunity to return.* 16 But as it is, they desire a better country, that is, a heavenly one. Therefore God is not ashamed to be called their God, for he has prepared for them a city. (Heb. 11:13-16; emphasis mine)

In this covenant God promises Abraham descendants as well as a place for his descendants to dwell. God is expanding the details of the covenant made in Eden. The promised offspring will cause many sons (both biological as well as from the nations) to be raised up for Abraham, and this offspring will cause them to inherit the land forever (Gen. 13:15; Heb. 9:15). God's covenant in eternity will be carried out in history through Abraham.

Understandably, Abraham wants to know how he can be certain all these promises will come to be. How can he know for sure that he will possess the land? If God is promising a new heavens and earth (Heb. 11:15-16), a place where righteousness dwells, then let's face it; such a holy place for a holy people is simply out of Abraham's reach. It is out of his descendants reach because he knows that he is not holy and righteous and neither will they be. So how can he know that he will possess this land that is being promised? You see the covenant that God makes is not a sterile, legal contract. The covenant provides comfort. It provides assurance, and it lays our doubts to rest in the tomb where Christ's body was laid. The Abrahamic covenant is about our Lord Jesus Christ.

Abraham's sons will only be able to receive the promised inheritance one way: through faith.[6] In faith (Gen. 15:6), Abraham seeks understanding, "O Lord God, how am I to know that I shall possess it?"

> [9] He said to him, "Bring me a heifer three years old, a female goat three years old, a ram three years old, a turtledove, and a young pigeon." [10] And he brought him all these, cut them in half, and laid each half over against the other. But he did not cut the birds in half. [11] And when birds of prey came down on the carcasses, Abram drove them away. (Gen. 15:9-11)

The way that Abraham responds to the Lord is fascinating. God said bring me these animals, and Abraham not only brings them, he sacrifices them and puts the severed parts across from one another. When God tells him to bring these animals, Abraham knows what God is going to do. He is going to enter into a solemn covenant with Abraham. There is an ancient covenant preserved from the eighth century BC. This was a treaty that Ashurnirari V (then king of Assyria) made with the Mati'ilu, King of Arpad:

> This ram is not brought from his herd for sacrifice, nor is he brought out for a garitu-festival, nor is he brought out for a kinitu-festival, nor is he brought out for (a rite for) a sick man, nor is he brought out for slaughter a[s. . . .] It is to make the treaty of Ashumirari, King of Assyria, with Mati'ilu that he is brought out. If Mati'ilu [sins] against the treaty sworn by the gods, just as this ram is broug[ht here] from his herd and to his herd will not return [and stand] at its head, so may Mati'ilu with his sons, [his nobles,] the people of his land [be brought] far from his land and to his land not return [to stand] at the head of his land.

---

[6] What is true faith? True faith is not only a knowledge and conviction that everything God reveals in his Word is true; it is also a deep-rooted assurance, created in me by the Holy Spirit through the gospel that, out of sheer grace earned for us by Christ, not only others, but I too, have had my sins forgiven, have been made forever right with God, and have been granted salvation. (Heidelberg Catechism Lord's Day 7, Q/A 21)

> This head is not the head of a ram; it is the head of Mati'ilu, the head of his sons, his nobles, the people of his land. If those named [sin] against this treaty, as the head of this ram is c[ut off,] his leg put in his mouth [. . .] so may the head of those named be cut off [. . . .] This shoulder is not the shoulder of a ram, it is the shoulder of the one named, it is the shoulder of [his sons, his nobles], the people of his land. If Mati'ilu sins against this treaty, as the shou[lder of this ram] is torn out, [. . .] so may the [shoulder of the one na]med, [his] sons, [his nobles,] the people of [his land] be torn out [. . .][7]

In this ritual a ram is brought out from the herd. Its head is removed which symbolized the fate of Mati'ilu should he break the covenant. This practice of animal sacrifice when commitments are made, dramatically acting out what would take place if one fails to live up to the terms of the agreement, is widely attested in the ancient world, particularly during the time of Abraham. This is probably why no mention is made of Abraham being instructed as to what to do.

What many scholars have pointed out is the similar covenant ceremony that takes place about 1,400 years later in Israel's history. In Jeremiah 34 the Lord promises to punish Israel for her sins. The king of Babylon was coming up against the city of Jerusalem because God had determined to make an end of the city. Why? Well the book of Jeremiah is filled with lots of details about the sins of the people. Jeremiah 34 focuses upon Israel's refusal to let their Hebrew slaves go. In the law of God, after the seven-year cycle, Hebrew slaves were to be released. This was not taking place, and so King Zedekiah, in an attempt to forestall the judgments that were pronounced against the city, called for the release of all the Hebrew slaves.

God approved of this decision because it was prescribed in his law. But the people ended up doing more than just letting the slaves go. That would have been enough, but they added something to the release. The Lord reminds them, "…you made a covenant before me in the house that is called by my name" (Jer. 34:15). They made a covenant and they bound themselves to this commitment. But it was a commitment that they broke. They took back their Hebrew slaves violating the covenant that they made, and in return God pronounced judgment:

> [17] "Therefore, thus says the Lord: You have not obeyed me by proclaiming liberty, every one to his brother and to his

---

[7] M.G. Kline, *By Oath Consigned* (Grand Rapids: Eerdmans, 1968), 41.

> neighbor; behold, I proclaim to you liberty to the sword, to pestilence, and to famine, declares the Lord. I will make you a horror to all the kingdoms of the earth. [18]And the men who transgressed my covenant and did not keep the terms of the covenant that they made before me, I will make them like the calf that they cut in two and passed between its parts— [19]the officials of Judah, the officials of Jerusalem, the eunuchs, the priests, and all the people of the land who passed between the parts of the calf. [20]And I will give them into the hand of their enemies and into the hand of those who seek their lives. Their dead bodies shall be food for the birds of the air and the beasts of the earth." (Jer. 34:17-20)

He held them accountable for the oath they swore when the covenant was made. All the people, great and small, walked between the severed calf which sealed their commitment, "May I become like this calf if I break this covenant and take my slaves back." The response from heaven in essence was, "so be it." They took their slaves back, and "they profaned the name of God" (Jer. 34:16). How so? It was because the very idea of the release of Hebrew slaves every seventh year was a perpetual reminder that God saved Israel from the land of slavery. God promised Abraham in Genesis 15 that his offspring would go into slavery and that God would bring them out again. He kept his word. He brought them up from the house of bondage; therefore, every Israelite slave owner was to release his Hebrew slave in celebration of God's deliverance of His people. To fail to do this was to fail to honor God. It was to disown him as Lord, and it was a rejection of the goodness that he had shown to his people when he set them free.

Covenants were not to be entered into halfheartedly. These covenants meant life or death. Now you can imagine what could have been going through Abraham's mind. He is shrouded in darkness, and this darkness creates dread and probably fear in him. It is an unnatural darkness. It begins to grip his soul as he looks at the carnage of the severed animals sitting across from one another. He has made the pathway in blood. Would Abraham have to walk down it? What duty would be required of him in order for this covenant to be fulfilled? What must *he* do in order to be the one through whom the blessings to the world would come? He must have shuddered at the thought. But then something unexpected happens:

> [17] When the sun had gone down and it was dark, behold, a smoking fire pot and a flaming torch passed between these pieces. [18] On that day the Lord made a covenant with Abram" (Gen. 15:17-18)

This, like the covenant of Genesis 3:15, will be a covenant of sheer grace.[8] God passed through the carnage alone and swore the oath upon the pain of death. Now the critical issue is, how will God do it and this is why we said that the word *offspring* can be *one* or *many*. God is going to save the many offspring through one particular offspring.

On one level this is fulfilled four hundred years later. Four hundred years go by, and the offspring of Abraham are in bondage. God raised up one particular offspring who would deliver them, namely, Moses. And before the last book of the Torah[9] closes, the Abrahamic promises are reviewed and reapplied to his descendants. Before Israel enters the Promised Land, Moses blesses the offspring of Abraham by drawing on words found in Genesis 15:

Gen. 15:1 I am Your shield
Deut. 33:29 a people saved by the Lord, the shield of your help

Gen. 15:2, Eliezer = God is help
Deut. 33:7, O Lord… be a help against his (Judah's) adversaries

Gen. 15:4 one from your own body will be your heir
Deut. 33:23, the blessing of the Lord, possess the lake and the south. (same word)

Gen. 15:6 and he counted it to him as righteousness
Deut. 33:21, with Israel he executed the righteousness of the Lord

Gen. 15:7 to give you this land to possess
Deut. 33:28, in a land of grain and wine, whose heavens drop down dew

Gen. 15:14 I will judge the nation that they serve
Deut. 33:22, Dan is a lion's cub (Dan = "God is judge")

Gen. 15:18 On that day the Lord made a covenant with Abram

---

[8] The manifestations of God's presence, a smoking fire pot and flaming torch, are similar to his later appearance to Israel at Mt Sinai. "Now Mount Sinai was wrapped in smoke because the Lord had descended on it in fire. The smoke of it went up like the smoke of a kiln" (Ex. 19:18).

[9] The Torah, or "Pentateuch" is the 5 books of Moses (Genesis-Deuteronomy).

Deut. 33:9 For they observed your word and kept your <u>covenant</u>[10]

Moses drew out the important elements of God's promise to Abraham, and he used them to pronounce the blessing on Abraham's descendants who were now a mighty nation. Moses blessed Israel, and in chapter 34 the Pentateuch ends with the death of Moses and the beginning of his successor, Joshua, filled with the spirit of wisdom (v. 9). But this, too, was a type and shadow of something greater.

It is not until we arrive at the Gospels that we see the fullness of what God was promising Abraham. Christ is the offspring of Abraham (Matt. 1:1ff.). Christ delivers Abraham's many offspring. Christ Jesus is the one who delivers from the greater dangers: Satan, sin, death, and hell. Christ's death is the greater death that breaks the greater bondage. Because of the death, burial, and resurrection of this offspring, the many offspring can receive the covenant blessings of Abraham and enter into paradise, their eternal inheritance.

Paul says that "the promises were made to Abraham and to his offspring. It does not say, 'And to offsprings,' referring to many, but referring to one, 'And to your offspring,' who is Christ" (Gal. 3:16). In Abraham, Jesus was contemplated as *the* offspring, and Paul makes this incredible connection between Abraham's Son and you:

> [26] for in Christ Jesus you are all sons of God, through faith. [27] For as many of you as were baptized into Christ have put on Christ. [28] There is neither Jew nor Greek, there is neither slave nor free, there is no male and female, for you are all one in Christ Jesus. [29] And if you are Christ's, then you are Abraham's offspring, heirs according to promise. (Gal. 3:26-29)

When God brought Abraham outside of his tent and told him, "Look up into the sky, look at all the stars that are there, so shall your offspring be," he was showing Abraham you. As Abraham gazed up at the stars that lit up the night, he saw a preview of the many people who would find a place in Abraham's family, through Abraham's Son, Jesus. By faith in Jesus Christ, you are part of the fulfillment to that promise that God made to Abraham so long ago. Actually, it stretches back further still. In eternity, God the Father promised his Son that his offspring would be as numerous as the stars that Abraham would look up at and struggle to count. As lovers and followers of Jesus Christ, you are each a light in the darkness, promised to the Son by the Father. So let your light shine in the midst of this dark world by living lives of gratitude for his mercy in making you a son and daughter of Father Abraham.

---

[10] Sailhamer, *Meaning of the Pentateuch*, 452.

Chapter Four

Study Questions:

1. How is Abraham used in the covenant of grace?
2. Who will God bless through Abraham? Why? How?
3. In what ways are Abraham and Adam similar/different?
4. What does God promise to give Abraham in this covenant?
5. What was the symbolic meaning of the severed animals?
6. Why didn't Abraham walk through the animal parts?
7. How does the Abrahamic covenant point us to Christ?

Chapter 5: The Mosaic Covenant: The Need for a Covenant Keeper

Dying words, living faith

J. Gresham Machen lived in the early part of the twentieth century. He founded Westminster Theological Seminary and was instrumental in the formation of the Orthodox Presbyterian Church. His biographer, Ned Stonehouse, gives this account of his passing into glory:

> Dismissing his doctor's orders, J. Gresham Machen, beaten down by a career of struggling for the Faith even within his own communion, kept his commitments to a small circle of Orthodox Presbyterian parishes in South Dakota. "I have too much to do," he insisted, as his chest was even then tight from pneumonia. The next day, however, Machen was hospitalized. On New Year's Eve, the host pastor visited this infamous opponent of Liberalism on his deathbed and the elder statesman related a dream he had enjoyed that made him long for Heaven. "Sam, it was glorious, it was glorious," he said. "Sam, isn't the Reformed Faith grand?" Just before he passed into the next world, Machen dictated a telegram to John Murray, professor of systematic theology at Westminster Seminary. These last words read, "I'm so thankful for the active obedience of Christ. No hope without it."[1]

Theologians tend to summarize the life of Jesus in terms of his active and passive obedience. Active obedience is Christ's thirty-three years of perfect conformity to God's will. Passive obedience is his death upon the cross. These are broad categories, categories that should not be interpreted to mean that Jesus did not suffer in those thirty-three years.[2]

---

[1] Ned B. Stonehouse, *J. Gresham Machen: A Biographical Memoir* (Carlisle: Banner of Truth, 1977), 508.

[2] As the Heidelberg Catechism puts it in Lord's Day 15, What do you understand by the word "suffered?" That all the time He lived on earth, but especially at the end of His life, He bore, in body and soul, the wrath of God against the sin of the whole human race; in order that by His suffering, as the only atoning sacrifice, He might redeem our body and soul from everlasting damnation, and obtain for us the grace of God, righteousness, and eternal life.

Nor does it mean that he is a passive victim on the cross. He determined to go there, and he actively obeyed by staying there until the work was finished.

Back to Machen, why didn't he say, "I am so thankful for the passive obedience of Christ"? Machen, of course, believed that Christ's substitutionary atonement was necessary for his salvation. Machen's statement also identifies his conviction that a forgiven sinner still has need of the righteousness that God requires, the righteousness of Christ (Phil. 3:9). That righteousness cannot be earned; it can only be received by faith and not by works. We need not only the holy death of Jesus. We need the righteous life of Jesus to fulfill the law's demands.

How the Mosaic covenant connects to the previous covenants

The Mosaic covenant was made with Israel in order to teach the nation about the grace and the justice of God. The Mosaic covenant taught Israel that they needed someone not only to stand in their place and offer a perfect sacrifice on their behalf; they also needed someone to stand in their place and be their perfect law-keeper. The Mosaic covenant was an administration of the covenant of grace as the Lord pointed his people to his redeemer, Jesus Christ. No one in this covenant is saved by their own law keeping (Rom. 9:31-33). The children of Abraham could only be saved in exactly the same way that Abraham was saved, by faith (Gal. 3:6-7).

Covenant theologians have also spoken of the Mosaic covenant as a republication of the covenant of works.[3] Of course grace does not end when the Mosaic covenant begins. And yet the Mosaic covenant is put into place to teach Israel that the covenant of works still needed to be kept for the goal to be reached. As we learned in the covenant of works, the goal is nothing less than God's throne in the midst of God's glorified people in God's land (i.e. the new heavens and earth).

When Adam failed to live in perfect obedience to God's commands, God didn't say, "Well that's unfortunate; therefore, I won't require righteous obedience since Adam and his descendants are incapable of it." In this covenant God was saying that obedience to all that he commands is still *required*. The Mosaic covenant teaches Israel about the grace of God as well as the righteous justice of God.

---

[3] For a detailed discussion of the doctrine of the republication of the covenant of works readers are encouraged to consult *The Law is Not of Faith,* Bryan D. Estelle, J. V. Fesko and David VanDrunen eds., (Phillipsburg, NJ: Presbyterian and Reformed, 2009)

As we look at the covenant made with Israel, we will consider three things:

1. Why there is grace in the Mosaic covenant
2. Why there are works in the Mosaic covenant
3. How this covenant furthers the covenant of grace made to Abraham and Adam before him

Why was there grace in the Mosaic covenant?

The most obvious answer is because without grace, no one would be saved. If there was no grace in this covenant, then none of the children of Israel would have been saved. Moses, Aaron, Joshua, Rahab, Ruth, the prophet Samuel, King David, Elijah, and many others would have been cast into hell if there was no grace operative in the Mosaic covenant. So even though we talk and think about the Mosaic covenant as a covenant of law, that does not mean that grace is absent. There are many examples of God's grace in this covenant made with Israel at Mount Sinai.

The preface to the Ten Commandments teaches Israel about the grace of God. "I am the Lord your God, who brought you out of the land of Egypt, out of the house of bondage" (Ex. 20:2). The promises of God are lessons in grace:

> And the Lord your God will circumcise your heart and the heart of your offspring, so that you will love the Lord your God with all your heart and with all your soul, that you may live. (Deut. 30:6)

The prophecies given to Israel are gracious expectations:

> I will raise up for them a prophet like you from among their brothers. And I will put my words in his mouth, and he shall speak to them all that I command him. (Deut. 18:18)

The sacrifices were constant reminders of God's commitment to show Israel grace:

> And he shall bathe his body in water in a holy place and put on his garments and come out and offer his burnt offering and the burnt offering of the people and make atonement for himself and for the people. (Lev. 16:24)

The feasts of Israel were especially appropriate reminders of God's grace and love:

> [39] On the fifteenth day of the seventh month, when you have gathered in the produce of the land, you shall celebrate the feast of the Lord seven days. On the first day shall be a solemn

rest, and on the eighth day shall be a solemn rest. ⁴⁰ And you shall take on the first day the fruit of splendid trees, branches of palm trees and boughs of leafy trees and willows of the brook, and you shall rejoice before the Lord your God seven days. ⁴¹ You shall celebrate it as a feast to the Lord for seven days in the year. It is a statute forever throughout your generations; you shall celebrate it in the seventh month. ⁴² You shall dwell in booths for seven days. All native Israelites shall dwell in booths, ⁴³ that your generations may know that I made the people of Israel dwell in booths when I brought them out of the land of Egypt: I am the Lord your God. (Lev. 23:39-43)

The Westminster Confession nicely summarizes the gracious work of God during the Mosaic covenant:

> This covenant [of grace] was differently administered in the time of the law, and in the time of the gospel: under the law, it was administered by promises, prophecies, sacrifices, circumcision, the paschal lamb, and other types and ordinances delivered to the people of the Jews, all foresignifying Christ to come; which were, for that time, sufficient and efficacious, through the operation of the Spirit, to instruct and build up the elect in faith in the promised Messiah, by whom they had full remission of sins, and eternal salvation; and is called the old testament. (WCF 7.5)

The time of the Law did not provide another way for Israel to be saved. Through the ceremonies and the sacrifices performed in the tabernacle, God was strengthening the faith of his Old Testament people with the same covenant grace that he administers to his people today through the proclamation of the gospel and the administration of the sacraments. The Spirit of God was working through those means to apply the promised grace of God (Gen. 3:15) to his elect people. As Charles Hodge remarked:

> We have the direct authority of the New Testament for believing that the covenant of grace, or plan of salvation, thus underlay the whole of the institutions of the Mosaic period, and that their principal design was to teach through types and symbols what is now taught in explicit terms in the gospel. Moses, we are told (Heb. iii. 5), was faithful as a servant to testify concerning the things which were to be spoken after.[4]

---

[4] Charles Hodge, *Systematic Theology*, 3 vols. (Grand Rapids: Eerdnams, 1997), 2.375.

The covenant of grace was operative in the time of the Mosaic covenant. Anyone who would say that Israelites were saved in any way other than grace is simply not a Christian. God was showing Israel by prophecies, sacrifices, and ceremonies that he remained committed to the promises that he made to Abraham and Adam before him. Perhaps one of the most graphic reminders of the depths of God's love and grace is the way God chose Israel:

> [1] Again the word of the Lord came to me: [2] "Son of man, make known to Jerusalem her abominations, [3] and say, Thus says the Lord God to Jerusalem: Your origin and your birth are of the land of the Canaanites; your father was an Amorite and your mother a Hittite. [4] And as for your birth, on the day you were born your cord was not cut, nor were you washed with water to cleanse you, nor rubbed with salt, nor wrapped in swaddling cloths. [5] No eye pitied you, to do any of these things to you out of compassion for you, but you were cast out on the open field, for you were abhorred, on the day that you were born. [6] "And when I passed by you and saw you wallowing in your blood, I said to you in your blood, 'Live!' I said to you in your blood, 'Live!' (Ezek. 16:1-6)

God's description of the way in which he found the nation removes any pretense from them of self-worth and importance. What a moving account of the tender mercies of God. No one would pity this nation as it lay, barely birthed, wallowing in its own blood. But God breathed life into them and took them to be his own treasured possession.

He did that because of his love and grace, nothing more, nothing less. His kindness to the nation of Israel was not because of what they could offer but because of the oath God had sworn to their fathers to give them the land that flowed with milk and honey (Ex. 13:5). God fulfilled this word to the patriarchs by bringing the Israelites out of Egypt, and he fulfilled his word by bringing them into the Promised Land of Canaan. As they lived in the land of Canaan, they were reminded of his grace in things like Passover, circumcision, and sacrifices. But works were also *required* in the Mosaic covenant.

Why was there works in the Mosaic covenant?

Why does God require works of Israel in this covenant arrangement? God required the work of obedience to drive Israel to despair and to seek the grace of God. Secondly, the works required in this covenant taught Israel what the faithful Son of God would do on their behalf in order to bring them to the eternal Promised Land. Works are in the Mosaic covenant to show Israel that perfect conformity to the will of God was unquestionably necessary. Israel was being called upon to place their faith and confidence in the one whom God would raise up. In that time and in various ways (Heb. 1:1), God was showing Israel that the Messiah, Jesus, would faithfully do all that they failed to do. The obedience required of the nation provided a picture of the obedient second Adam, of whom Israel was only a type.

Another Adam-like figure

During the time of the Mosaic covenant, the law underscored Israel's desperate need for grace. On a typological level, it was a reminder of the broken covenant of works with Adam and it created an eager expectation as it pointed forward to the time when Christ would fulfill all the law's demands. The strict legal requirements, the demands for obedience as a condition for staying in the Promised Land, and the threats of being cursed have persuaded various covenant theologians to interpret the time of the Law as a republication of the covenant of works.[5] On the level of type and shadow, Israel as a nation is a corporate Adam. Sinful though they were, they bore a resemblance to their covenant head who himself broke fellowship with God.

---

[5] For an examination of the various forms of Republication see Brenton C. Ferry, "Works in the Mosaic Covenant," in Bryan D. Estelle, J. V. Fesko and David VanDrunen eds., *The Law is Not of Faith* (Phillipsburg, NJ: Presbyterian and Reformed, 2009), 76-108. Francis Turretin, *Institutes of Elenctic Theology*, 3 vols. (Philipsburg, NJ: Presbyterian & Reformed, 1994), 2:263; Edward Fisher, The Marrow of Modern D*ivinity* (Geanies House, Fearn, Tain, Ross-shire: Christian Focus, 2009), 45-62; Herman Witsius, *The Economy of the Covenants Between God and Man*, 2 vols. (1822; Philipsburg, NJ: Presbyterian and Reformed, 1990), 2:182-183. James Buchanan, *The Doctrine of Justification: An Outline of its History in the Church and of its Exposition from Scripture* (Carlisle: The Banner of Truth Trust, 1991) 39. John Colquhoun, *A Treatise on the Law and the Gospel* (Grand Rapids, MI: Soli Deo Gloria Publications, 2009), 55-75. Jonathan Edwards, *The Works of President Edwards: With a memoir of His Life*, 10 vols. (New York: S. Converse, 1829) 3:211; Geerhardus Vos, Redemptive History and Biblical Interpretation (Philipsburg, NJ: Presbyterian & Reformed, 1980), 255. Meredith Kline, God Heaven and Har Magedon (Eugene, OR: Wipf & Stock, 2006), 128-129. Charles Hodge once wrote, "It said, 'Do this and live... it contained, as does also the New Testament, a renewed proclamation of the original covenant of works." Hodge, *Systematic Theology*, 2:375.

There are a number of parallels that exist between Adam and the nation of Israel.[6] God created Adam outside the Garden of Eden and placed him in it; Israel was created outside of Canaan and brought into it (Ex.33:16-17, Joel 2:3). Adam is called God's son (Lk. 3:38, Gen. 5:1-3), Israel's relationship to God is that of a son (Ex. 4:22-23, Hos. 11:1). The themes of being fruitful and multiplying are applied to Adam (Gen. 1:22) and Israel (Ex. 1:7). Adam was given the law (Gen. 2:17), so also Israel (Ex. 19ff.). Under the sign of the Tree of Life and the Sabbath, Adam was promised life for his obedience. Israel was also promised life for obedience to God's commands (Lev. 18:5). The curse of death for disobedience was declared to Adam (Gen. 2:17) and Israel (Deut. 30:19). The remembrance of Adam is renewed and revived in Israel (Rom. 5:14ff.).

The covenant with Israel also bears some resemblance to the covenant of works with Adam. In Exodus 19 we find Israel at the foot of Mount Sinai. God then gives Moses the conditions of the covenant that he is about to make with Israel:

> Now therefore, if you will indeed obey my voice and keep my covenant, you shall be my treasured possession among all peoples. (Ex. 19:5)

This is what Moses is to tell Israel. The terms and conditions are not optional. If you want to be God's treasured possession, then you must obey the Lord's voice and keep his covenant. How does Israel respond?

> [7] So Moses came and called the elders of the people and set before them all these words that the Lord had commanded him. [8] All the people answered together and said, "All that the Lord has spoken we will do." And Moses reported the words of the people to the Lord. (Ex. 19:7-8)

The terms of the covenant are to obey God's voice, and Israel says, "we will do it all." I sometimes wonder if Moses was tempted to roll his eyes when Israel swore obedience. They were complaining before they left Egypt and crossed the sea. They grumbled against the Lord on the way to the mountainside. They murmured about the water at Marah. They said they would rather be back in Egypt where they had meat, so God gave them quail. God gave them manna and told them to gather a double portion on the sixth day and rest on the seventh, but some

---

[6] *Dictionary of Biblical Imagery*, eds. T. Leland Ryken, James C. Wilhoit, Tremper Longman III (Leicester: Inter-Varsity Press, 1998), 12. Greg Beale, *A New Testament Biblical Theology* (Grand Rapids: Baker, 2011), 91.

disobeyed and went looking for it on the Sabbath– already a strong indicator of their incapacity for obedience. A little farther into the wilderness, and the people were at it again, lamenting over the lack of water. There were signs long before the incident of the golden calf that Israel was anything but a faithful covenant partner.

In Exodus 20-23 God gave Moses the law of the covenant, and in the twenty-forth chapter we have the people's response:

> [3] Moses came and told the people all the words of the Lord and all the rules. And all the people answered with one voice and said, "All the words that the Lord has spoken we will do."

> [6] And Moses took half of the blood and put it in basins, and half of the blood he threw against the altar. Then he took the Book of the Covenant and read it in the hearing of the people. And they said, "All that the Lord has spoken we will do, and we will be obedient." And Moses took the blood and threw it on the people and said, "Behold the blood of the covenant that the Lord has made with you in accordance with all these words."

In this covenant with Israel, the Lord gathers his people to his holy mountain, and there he declares that he is the king and if they would live long in his land, they must obey all of his laws, statutes, and commandments. Three times Israel says, "All that the Lord has spoken we will do."

God binds Adam to the covenant, requiring of him obedience to the law upon the threat of death. Israel must swear to do *all* that God commands, and the blood is sprinkled on them. This symbolizes that if they break their word and fail to live according to the law of this covenant, then they will become like the bull that was slain. From this vantage point, the covenant with Israel resembles the covenant of works.

The duties required to retain the possession of the land also remind us of the covenant of works:

> [25] When you father children and children's children, and have grown old in the land, if you act corruptly by making a carved image in the form of anything, and by doing what is evil in the sight of the Lord your God, so as to provoke him to anger, [26] I call heaven and earth to witness against you today, that you will soon utterly perish from the land that you are going over the Jordan to possess. You will not live long in it, but will be utterly destroyed. (Deut. 4:25-26)

Deuteronomy 30 especially highlights the privilege of living in the land as being connected with obedience and life:

> [17] But if your heart turns away, and you will not hear, but are drawn away to worship other gods and serve them, [18] I declare to you today, that you shall surely perish. You shall not live long in the land that you are going over the Jordan to enter and possess. [19] I call heaven and earth to witness against you today, that I have set before you life and death, blessing and curse. Therefore choose life, that you and your offspring may live, [20] loving the Lord your God, obeying his voice and holding fast to him, for he is your life and length of days, that you may dwell in the land that the Lord swore to your fathers, to Abraham, to Isaac, and to Jacob, to give them. (Deut. 30:17-20)

Israel's tenure in the land was conditioned upon obedience to the commands of God (Lev. 18:26-28; Lev. 20:22). While not immediately removed at the first violation, on the typological level this arrangement does resemble the covenant of works made with Adam. If this corporate Adam disobeys, they, like Adam before them, will be cast out of the beautiful land God had given to them.

As the history of Israel unfolds and unravels, the prophet Hosea registers his judicial complaint against God's sinful and rebellious covenant partners, reminding them that they are following in Adam's footsteps:[7]

> But like Adam they transgressed the covenant; there they dealt faithlessly with me. (Hos. 6:7)

The apostle Paul likewise draws a comparison between Adam and Israel's failure to do what God commands and then contrasts both with Christ's sinless obedience:

> [12] Therefore, just as sin came into the world through one man, and death through sin, and so death spread to all men because all sinned— [13] for sin indeed was in the world before the law was given, but sin is not counted where there is no law. [14] Yet death reigned from Adam to Moses, even over those whose

---

[7] B. B. Warfield, "Hosea VI. 7: Adam or Man?" in *Selected Shorter Writings of Benjamin B. Warfield*, 2 vols. (Phillipsburg NJ: Presbyterian & Reformed, 1970), 1.116-29. Byron G. Curtis, "Hosea 6:7 and Covenant-Breaking Like/at Adam," in *The Law is Not of Faith*, 170-209.

sinning was not like the transgression of Adam, who was a type of the one who was to come. (Rom. 5:12-14)

Paul proved that sin was in the world between the time of Adam and Moses because people died (cf. Rom. 6:23). People were sinning between the time of Adam and Moses, but not in a way *like* Adam. Adam's sin was of a particular kind. It was a violation of the covenant of works. We observe that there is a subtle reference to this particular type of sinning (a covenant violation) in the second half of v. 14. Death reigned from Adam to Moses, even over those whose sinning was *not* like the transgression of Adam. But when the covenant under Moses is made, then national sinning is *like* the transgression of Adam. This reading of Romans 5:14 lends further support to the Old Testament lines of correspondence that we have pointed out between Adam and Israel. Adam's sin was of a distinct kind. The sins that were committed after Adam's covenant transgression were not analogous. But once Israel enters into covenant with God, the sins that follow are *like* that of Adam in covenant with God. Adam is told that he can eat from any tree in the garden. The Tree of Life was offered to him upon one condition; he must not eat from the Tree of the Knowledge of Good and Evil. To choose to eat from that tree was to choose death. On a typological level, Israel's relationship with God is a republication of the covenant of works:

> I call heaven and earth to witness against you today, that I have set before you life and death, blessing and curse. Therefore choose life, that you and your offspring may live. (Deut. 30:19)

It is also important to note that like Adam, Israel's obedience or lack thereof affected their offspring (Ex. 22:24; Lev. 26:22; Deut. 4:40; 11:19-21; 12:25, 28). They are threatened with the curse and death and are commanded to choose life so that they and their offspring might live. And what does choosing life look like?

> ...loving the Lord your God, obeying his voice and holding fast to him, for he is your life and length of days, that you may dwell in the land that the Lord swore to your fathers, to Abraham, to Isaac, and to Jacob, to give them. (Deut. 30:20)

The obedience required of Israel is not something that they can achieve: This prescribed obedience made the elect Israelites long for that obedience to be secured for them by another. This is what makes Jesus exceedingly precious. This is why Machen could say the words that he did. Jesus is the true Son of God, the obedient Adam and faithful Israel. Having grasped that the covenant with Israel was to teach them about faithful Jesus in covenant with God, we turn to yet one more function of the law for the life of the believer.

A guide to gratitude

The law is also our guide, revealing to us how to please the Lord. In this regard the law serves two functions. It is a perfect rule for obtaining righteousness and life. This in turn brings us to despair. Our sins are exposed by the law. Our consciences condemn us that we have not kept it. The overwhelming guilt of offending the holy God of heaven and earth would shackle us in despair and hopelessness forever were it not for the gospel, the good news that Christ has redeemed us from the curse of the law by becoming a curse for us (Gal. 3:13). How then can we live a life of thankfulness to God for sending his Son to rescue us from eternal condemnation? We go to his word to find out what pleases him and seek his help to do that which he approves.[8] The law is not useless for the believer; it is our guide to gratitude. The Westminster Confession of Faith lays out the relationship between the law and the believer:

> Although true believers be not under the law as a covenant of works, to be thereby justified or condemned; yet is it of great use to them, as well as to others; in that, as a rule of life, informing them of the will of God and their duty, it directs and binds them to walk accordingly; discovering also the sinful pollutions of their nature, hearts, and lives; so as, examining themselves thereby, they may come to further conviction of, humiliation for, and hatred against sin; together with a clearer sight of the need they have of Christ, and the perfection of His obedience. (WCF. 19.6)

To those who are not united to Christ, the law condemns, yet to those united to Christ, it points the way to thankful living in the freedom that Christ has won for us (1 Tim. 1:8).[9] David delighted in God's mercy:

> [2] Bless the Lord, O my soul,

---

[8] What is the coming-to-life of the new self? It is wholehearted joy in God through Christ and a delight to do every kind of good as God wants us to. What do we do that is good? Only that which arises out of true faith, conforms to God's law, and is done for his glory; and not that which is based on what we think is right or on established human tradition. (Heidelberg Catechism Lord's Day 33, Q/A 90-91)

[9] For an excellent and wonderfully balanced exposition of the law as our guide for showing gratitude see, Fisher, *The Marrow of Modern Divinity*.

> and forget not all his benefits,
>
> ³ who forgives all your iniquity,
>
> who heals all your diseases,
>
> ⁴ who redeems your life from the pit,
>
> who crowns you with steadfast love and mercy
>
> (Ps. 103:2-4)

It was because of God's kindness and grace that the king of Israel could say, "I love thy law" (Ps. 119:165). It would be a serious mistake to think that we can come up with our own way of pleasing the Lord. The only way redeemed sinners can know what is good and what pleases the Lord is by his word. His word contains the sentence of condemnation that hung over us, the promise of salvation that was carried out for us, the assurance of pardon that is guaranteed to us, and the way of thankfulness to be lived out through the Holy Spirit he has given us. The heart of faith will be discernible by the life of gratitude, which is guided by the law.

Typology

When theologians talk about the covenant of works being republished in the Mosaic covenant, they are talking about typology. Various things and events in the Old Testament were types and shadows of the Savior. Jesus is the reality in his person *and in his work*. Try to think of it this way:

Circumcision

When the priests circumcised an infant male on the eighth day, that circumcision was a type. It was a copy that could never regenerate a person and make them born again. It pointed to the reality that through Jesus, God would circumcise the hearts of his people so that they would be born again.

The sacrificial lamb

The sacrificial lamb was the copy that could never take away sins. Jesus is the true Lamb of God who takes away the sins of the world.

Israel's temple

Israel's earthly temple and tabernacle were a type of God's heavenly temple. The earthly temple and tabernacle taught them about the heavenly temple of God.

Israel's obedience

Israel's obedience to the law was also a type that could never be rewarded with eternal life in the Promised Land. Jesus' obedience to the law is the reality that is rewarded with eternal life in the new heavens and earth.

In this covenant we would not want to say that Israel's obedience merited eternal life in the Promised Land any more than we would want to say that Israel's sacrifices covered their sins. Yet on the level of type/shadow, they are commanded to be obedient and commanded to offer the sacrifices because both things pointed to the active and passive obedience of Christ. Christ takes upon himself the covenant of works so that the covenant of grace could be given to us!

Therefore, we have the covenant of grace running through this covenant with Israel, and we have a republication of the covenant of works as well, both of which are pointing to Christ, but in different ways. Now we need to say something about our third point.

How does this covenant further the covenant of grace made to Abraham and Adam?

How does this covenant expand the promises made to Abraham? Let's look again at Exodus 19:5:

> Now therefore, if you will indeed obey my voice and keep my covenant, you shall be my treasured possession among all peoples, for all the earth is mine

There is a note of conditionality. *If* Israel obeys, *then* they will be God's treasure. But what about the words, "...for the whole world is mine"? If you consult the NIV, it is translated "...although the whole world is mine." Although the world is mine, I have chosen you Israel. This translation gives the impression that God could have chosen the whole world to be his, but he will be content with Israel. Translations such as the ESV, NKJV, and NASB translate it "for the whole earth is mine." I believe this translation captures the correct meaning, namely that God has chosen Israel for a greater purpose. God is concerned about the world, and Israel will be the people through whom he will rescue the world. To use a different way of speaking, Israel is to be a light to the nations. This is the promise to Abraham, "in you shall all the families of the world be blessed." Israel will be the special nation that God is going to use to reach the nations. The nations are not an afterthought in the mind of God. All along, Israel existed to be the conduit of God's light, welcoming the nations to find refuge in his grace. God's plan has always been a global plan. How do we know that this is the correct way of reading Exodus 19:5? We must read vv. 5-6 together to get this picture of the fullness of God's covenant people:

> Now therefore, if you will indeed obey my voice and keep my covenant, you shall be my treasured possession among all peoples, for all the earth is mine; [6] and you shall be to me a kingdom of priests and a holy nation. These are the words that you shall speak to the people of Israel. (Ex. 19:5)

In this covenant with God, they will be two things, a kingdom of priests, and a holy nation. What does it mean that Israel is collectively "a kingdom of priests"? We need to look no further than the Levitical priesthood. God separates the tribe of Levi out from among the other tribes of Israel. A priest is separated out from the people. God separates Israel from the nations. What is the priest's role? It is to represent the people to God and God to the people.

God puts Israel in Canaan. They are surrounded on every side by nations living estranged from God. In doing so the Lord is calling upon Israel to represent him to the nations (Isa. 61:6), to bring the nations to him. Through this one priestly nation, the nations of the world can approach God. The common nations of the world are to be served by the priestly nation of Israel as Israel obeys God. They are to love God and neighbor.

As the Bible goes on to show, Israel's history is often one of disobedience. Things pretty much go downhill fast, particularly in the book of Judges and after David and Solomon are laid to rest. It isn't always the case, but in general the nations of the world don't see the need to worship Israel's God. And so on this level of fulfillment, the Gentiles must wait in darkness until the day dawns when the faithful Son of Israel, Abraham, and Adam arrives.

One day, a baby was brought into the temple. And Simeon, who was waiting for the consolation of Israel, was led by the Spirit into the temple. His heart must have leapt with excitement as his eyes looked upon a young couple who had with them a little baby boy. It was as if the Spirit of God whispered into the old man's heart, "This is the one" (Lk. 2:22-32).

The old man took up the infant Jesus in his arms and said, "Lord, now you are letting your servant depart in peace." Now he is ready to go to his heavenly home. Now he can leave his land and his people in peace, "For my eyes have seen your salvation that you have prepared in the presence of all peoples, a light for revelation to the Gentiles, and for glory to your people Israel" (Lk. 2:29-32). But what does it take for Jesus to be "God's salvation"? What does it take for him to be a "light of revelation to the Gentiles"? What will it take for Jesus to be "Israel's glory"? It will take two things.

Active obedience

It will take nothing less than the active obedience of Christ. Jesus came to John in the River Jordan, and John was taken back and aghast. "What do you mean that you are coming to me to be baptized; I need to be baptized by you." And Jesus replied, "Let it be so now, for thus it is fitting for us to fulfill all righteousness." John's role in the fulfilling of all righteousness is to announce the coming of the Lord. He is the herald. He is the forerunner who announces and publicly identifies Jesus as the promised one to come. He is marked out as the beloved Son in whom the father is "well pleased" (Matt. 3:17). Jesus goes down into the waters which symbolized the judgment of God in the time of Noah and the washing and renewing of the Holy Spirit in the age that has come. He entered into the work of the covenant, representing every elect sinner from the time of Adam and Eve until the end of time.

In this moment the Father is distinguishing and honoring the Son above everyone who had come before him and would come after him. Everyone depends upon him, both the saints above and those dwelling on earth below. Everything is riding upon him. One violation, one little infraction of God's law and the hope of the world is dashed. The weight of the world is now placed upon his shoulders. Now he must do it. He must do what Adam failed to do. He must achieve what Israel could not accomplish. He must fulfill all righteousness by the labors of his hands, fulfilling God's law's demands.

Passive obedience

After living faithfully before God throughout his life, it will take nothing less than Christ's passive obedience to bring us into eternal life. There is one final labor of his hands that cause ours to tremble; those holy hands must be pierced. The justice of God demands it. Sin cannot go unpunished. The righteousness of God requires a full accounting of sins committed. And as the hymn teaches by song, it is here at the cross where:

> justice and mercy collide,
> there are on his hands and his feet and his side,
> come see how long and how deep and how wide,
> is the Father's love.[10]

God clothed Adam and Eve (Gen. 3:21); the soldiers stripped Jesus of his clothing (Jn. 19:24). Adam is the pinnacle of all that God had made (Gen. 1:26-30); Jesus is mocked as a pathetic nobody (Mk. 15:16-20).

---

[10] Song by Nathan Tasker, "Prone To Wander."

Adam was crowned with glory (Ps. 8:5); Jesus was crowned with a crown of thorns (Matt. 27:29). God put Adam in a beautiful garden (Gen. 2:15), and Jesus was put upon a cruel cross (Lk. 23:33). In the land once described as the Garden of the Lord, (Gen. 13:10) they crucified him. He hung upon that cross naked, a move by the Romans calculated to humiliate. The sins of God's sinful bride were imputed to Jesus. For every covenant violation, in word or in deed, Christ Jesus bled and died. With cold indifference, Adam said, "the woman who you gave me" (Gen. 3:12). In faithless self-protection, Abraham said of his wife, "she is my sister" (Gen. 12:19). Israel swears falsely, "all that the Lord commands we will do" (Ex. 24:3). These sins and more were imputed to Christ, and upon the cross the faithful covenant mediator cried out in agony, "Father forgive them they know not what they do (Lk. 23:34).

Here is the Second Adam, lifted up, crowned with the crown of thorns, the very sign of the curse: "Thorns and thistles it shall bring forth for you" (Gen. 3:18). Here is the dreaded darkness that fell upon Abraham as God passed through the severed animals: "And when the sixth hour had come, there was darkness over the whole land until the ninth hour" (Mk. 15:33). Luke is even more graphic, "the sun's light failed" (Lk. 23:45). The sun would give anything to give light to the one who gave it light, now hanging in agony and in darkness, but the sun's light failed because this darkness is the darkness of the judgment of God against his people's sins, now engulfing Christ on the cross.

"I have come to fulfill all righteousness" (Matt. 3:13). Those were the first words of Jesus entering into this covenant of works. "It is finished"—the final words of Jesus, securing for us the covenant of grace (Jn. 19:30).

Study Questions:

1. What did God teach Israel through the Mosaic covenant?

2. Why is the Mosaic covenant a part of the covenant of grace?
3. How does the Mosaic covenant reflect the covenant of works?
4. How is Israel like Adam?
5. What are the terms of this covenant? What must Israel do?
6. How does the law apply to Christians?
7. What does the Mosaic covenant teach us about Christ?

Chapter 6: The Davidic Covenant: The King Will Come

> Our modern usage, as it makes us think of the king almost exclusively under the aspect of a constitutional ruler and executive of the Law, more or less obscures the fact that to Israel the kingship was "a source of happiness, a foundation of blessing, a retreat for salvation: the kingship was a democratic institution. The king naturally took the part of the poor and oppressed, not of the powerful and violent; the king existed for the sake of Israel, not the reverse.[1]

A king for the kingdom

As we chart the course of history by means of the covenants, we have arrived at the covenant God made with David, a covenant that has much to do with God's royal house and God's royal son. If Abraham is held up as the man of faith (Heb. 11; Jas. 2) and Moses is the paradigm prophet (Acts 3:22), then David is surely Israel's greatest king. He is the warrior who slays Goliath, the commander who takes Jerusalem, the religious architect who receives the plans for building the temple. David's name appears in the headings of nearly half the psalms. He made musical instruments to be used for temple worship (1 Chron. 23:5). He ordered the worship in the temple (Ezr. 3:10). The twelve tribes prospered under David's reign. The faithfulness of kings are measured against David (1 Ki. 15:11; 2 Ki. 16:2). Mt. Zion bears the title "city of God" (Heb. 12:22) and is called "the city of David" (2 Sam. 5:7). David is a man after God's own heart (1 Sam. 13:14).[2]

What is the Davidic covenant?

The Davidic covenant is about the royal offspring/son of David who will

---

[1] Geerhardus Vos, *A Geerhardus Vos Anthoogy*, ed. Danny Olinger (Philipsburg, NJ: Presbyterian and Reformed, 2005), 175.

[2] M. L. Strauss, "David" in *New Dictionary of Biblical Theology*, ed. T. Desmond Alexander
and Brian S. Rosner (Leicester: Inter-Varsity Press, 2000), 435-443.

build the House of God and rule from his royal throne forever.

How the Davidic covenant connects with the covenants

How does the Davidic covenant connect and expand upon the covenants we have already covered? In the covenant of works, Adam must be perfectly obedient to earn eternal, glorified life in an un-fallen world with God's throne in the midst of his people. After Adam's failure to keep the terms of the covenant of works, God made a second covenant, the covenant of grace, in which he promised to deliver his people through one of their offspring. In the covenant with Noah, we learn that this offspring will be righteous; he will deliver his people from the flood of God's wrath and bring them into an earth cleansed from sin. The covenant with Abraham also takes up the matters of offspring and land. God promised to give Abraham an offspring (Gal. 3:16) who will be a blessing to the nations and will bring all God's elect people from every tongue, tribe, and nation into the Promised Land (Gal. 3:18). In the Mosaic covenant, the Lord delivered Abraham's offspring from the offspring of the serpent, Pharaoh. God entered into a covenant with Israel requiring faithfulness to all that he commanded them in order to enjoy his blessings in the Promised Land. They must do his commands (like Adam and Noah before them), and they must seek his grace (like Abraham) as they live in the Promised Land as a light to the nations. The covenant with Israel teaches us about the perfect obedience required of the promised offspring to possess the land of God's blessing.

The covenant with David connects to these covenants showing us that God will raise up for David an offspring who will rule over Israel forever. This is the same offspring promised to Adam and later to Abraham. This is the offspring who is righteous like Noah, who will be a blessing to the nations like Abraham, and who will build a house for God to dwell with his people forever. "In the Davidic covenant" writes O. Palmer Robertson, "God's purposes to redeem a people to himself reach their climactic stage of realization so far as the Old Testament is concerned. Under David the kingdom arrives."[3]

We will begin by looking at the context of the Davidic covenant and the elements of the covenant; namely offspring, a royal house and the eternal throne.

---

[3] O. Palmer Robertson, *The Christ of the Covenants* (Phillipsburg, NJ: Presbyterian and Reformed, 1980), 229. Cf. Bill Arnold, *1 & 2 Samuel* (Grand Rapids: Zondervan, 2003), 69.

Context

In 2 Samuel 6 the ark of the covenant arrives in Jerusalem. This was significant for a number of reasons. In the Bible, the ark of the covenant is closely connected to God's presence. God speaks with Moses from between the two cherubim which are on the ark (Ex. 25:18; Num. 7:89). The Lord sits enthroned above the cherubim (1 Chron. 13:6). The ark of the covenant is also referred to as the footstool of the Lord, the place where his holy feet rest (Ps. 132:7-8).

David's throne is established in Jerusalem, and the Lord graciously permits his throne to be relocated there as well. The Lord establishes David's rule in Jerusalem, and the Lord rules over and through the king in Jerusalem. In light of this special treatment, the excitement of David is an understandable reaction (2 Sam. 6:16). The relocation of the ark means that God has chosen to put his name in the City of David.[4]

God had previously indicated that he would not dwell in the tabernacle indefinitely:

> [5] But you shall seek the place that the Lord your God will choose out of all your tribes to put his name and make his habitation there. There you shall go, [6] and there you shall bring your burnt offerings and your sacrifices, your tithes and the contribution that you present, your vow offerings, your freewill offerings, and the firstborn of your herd and of your flock. (Deut. 12:5)[5]

Out of all the tribes of Israel, God chose the tribe of Judah. Of all the cities throughout the Promised Land, the Lord chose Jerusalem (1 Ki. 14:21; 2 Chron. 12:13). The divine rule is administered through David's rule and goes out from David's city.

The progression of God's promises

Not only is the Lord's special presence to be found in Jerusalem, his peace surrounds the city that he loves. 2 Samuel 7:1 opens with the hope that had been instilled into Israel right from the very beginning of world (cf. Gen. 2:2-3; Heb. 4:10-11):

> [1] Now when the king lived in his house and the Lord had given him rest from all his surrounding enemies...

The Lord gave David rest. His enemies were subdued. Israel was secure and the people were united around their king who ruled over the twelve tribes in the Promised Land. In the person of David, we get a

---

[4] City of David = Jerusalem (2 Sam. 5:7-9; 6:12-16).
[5] Cf. Deut. 16:2, 6-7, 15-16; 17:8-9; 18:6-7; 31:11.

CHAPTER SIX

clearer picture of Christ, and in the Davidic covenant we have all the elements of the previous covenants. Once again we are dealing with the subject of typology (Rom. 5:14; 1 Pet. 3:21). The king of Israel is raised up by the Lord to lift the expectations of his people, causing them to look for the arrival of the messianic king. David is the conqueror who defeats the offspring of the serpent. King David rescues Abraham's offspring from the hands of their enemies. They dwell in the Promised Land and enjoy peace and prosperity under a righteous king who lives according to the righteous commandments of God.[6] And perhaps most significantly, residing in the city of Jerusalem is the throne of God.

---

[6] As Rev. Clayton Willis reminded me, most people remember David primarily for his victory over Goliath and his failure with Bathsheba. To be sure these are significant and defining moments in the life of David, but they aren't the situations that the scriptures most reflect upon. David was saved by God's grace and preserved by God's grace because he was a sinner. He was also used to foreshadow the truly righteous king, Jesus, who would have no need of God's grace, God's de-merited favor. The *typological* connection between David and Christ can be seen in David's righteous obedience to the will of God which is underscored in numerous places. [21]"The Lord dealt with me according to my righteousness; according to the cleanness of my hands he rewarded me. [22] For I have kept the ways of the Lord and have not wickedly departed from my God. [23] For all his rules were before me, and from his statutes I did not turn aside. [24] I was blameless before him, and I kept myself from guilt. [24]And the Lord has rewarded me according to my righteousness, according to my cleanness in his sight. (2 Sam. 22:21-24) David's obedience to the commandments of God is elsewhere described affirmatively, "Nevertheless, I will not take the whole kingdom out of his hand, but I will make him ruler all the days of his life, for the sake of David my servant whom I chose, who kept my commandments and my statutes" (1 Ki. 11:34). That this assessment affirms only the typological level is clear from a later reference to David's sin(s) against Uriah, "because David did what was right in the eyes of the Lord and did not turn aside from anything that he commanded him all the days of his life, except in the matter of Uriah the Hittite" (1 Ki. 15:5). David's good deeds did not cancel out his bad deeds, earning him the title of righteous. David's righteousness was imputed to him by faith alone (Rom. 4:6). God used David for his redemptive purposes to give Israel a picture of the intrinsically righteous king whom David called, "Lord" (Psa. 110:1; Matt. 22:44-45).

As David is sitting in his palace enjoying his beautiful home and the peace and stability of the nation, he realizes something is not quite right. The king said to Nathan the prophet, "See now, I dwell in a house of cedar, but the ark of God dwells in a tent" (2 Sam. 7:2). This can't be right. David reasons that the great God who has so richly blessed him dwells in a tent while he lives in a house of cedar. If anything, it is backwards. And Nathan knows what David means. He gives David the go ahead, but then has to return and tell him that there is going to be a change of plan:

> ⁵ Go and tell my servant David, "Thus says the Lord: Would you build me a house to dwell in? ⁶ I have not lived in a house since the day I brought up the people of Israel from Egypt to this day, but I have been moving about in a tent for my dwelling. ⁷ In all places where I have moved with all the people of Israel, did I speak a word with any of the judges of Israel, whom I commanded to shepherd my people Israel, saying, "Why have you not built me a house of cedar?" (2 Sam. 7:5-7)

God dwelt in a tent, a mobile throne room, because his people were heading to Canaan. After entering the Promised Land, it took time before Canaan was subdued before them. But now that the Lord's people had rest and now that God's throne, the ark of the covenant, came to rest in Jerusalem, it made sense to David that *now* was the time for the temple-palace to be constructed. David was about to learn that he was not going to be able to build something for God, but God was going to build something for David. The Lord promised David offspring, a royal house and an eternal throne.

Offspring

The Davidic covenant shows the advancement of a major theme of the covenant of grace. The Lord said to David:

> When your days are fulfilled and you lie down with your fathers, I will raise up your offspring after you, who shall come from your body, and I will establish his kingdom. (2 Sam. 7:12)

That this covenantal promise is about offspring should come as no surprise. The Bible's own story line is built upon this expectation. The Davidic covenant further develops the Abrahamic covenant. Like Abraham, David will have an offspring who will come from his body. As David proposes to build the temple and is denied, so too Abraham proposed that the heir of his estate would be his servant, which was

Chapter Six

likewise rejected. "And behold, the word of the LORD came to him, saying, 'This one shall not be your heir, but one who will come from your own body shall be your heir.'" (Gen. 15:4 NKJV). The phrase, "from your own body" is identical to 2 Samuel 7:12. Abraham's offspring will come through David's offspring. Through the bloodline of Abraham and David comes the messianic king (Rom. 1:1-6), who receives the eternal kingdom (2 Sam. 7:13), whose rule will have no end (2 Sam. 7:16). An ancient prophecy announced the coming of such a king:

> [8] Judah, your brothers shall praise you; your hand shall be on the neck of your enemies; your father's sons shall bow down before you. [9] Judah is a lion's cub; from the prey, my son, you have gone up. He stooped down; he crouched as a lion and as a lioness; who dares rouse him? [10] The scepter shall not depart from Judah, nor the ruler's staff from between his feet, until tribute comes to him; and to him shall be the obedience of the peoples. [11] Binding his foal to the vine and his donkey's colt to the choice vine, he has washed his garments in wine and his vesture in the blood of grapes. [12] His eyes are darker than wine, and his teeth whiter than milk. (Gen. 49:8-12)

With prophetic insight, the old patriarch sees a day when the mighty warrior's hand will be on the neck of his enemies (v. 8), reverberating the promise of victory over the serpent's crushed head (Gen. 3:15). His brothers will bow down before him. He is exalted over all. The scepter will not depart from him. Tribute will come to him, and then there are the images of extravagance. This won't be a king who rules over a mediocre kingdom as the images of the donkey and washing the clothes make clear. What do you think would happen if you hitched a donkey to a grapevine? He's probably going to help himself to a little snack. You won't even have a vine left, let alone grapes. The picture here is one of abundance, of overabundance. There is so much produce that it would make no difference if your donkey ate until full. The donkey's colt is tied to the choice vine. Even the choicest vines are so plentiful that no one would even give a second thought to tying a young donkey to one of the choicest vines in the vineyard.

The second image is equally strange. Why would anyone wash their clothes in wine? The meaning is probably not to be found in a primitive form of dying clothes. Rather, the imagery communicates prosperity. The wine is so plentiful that it is as common as laundry water. What was the first miracle Jesus performed? He turned the water into wine (Jn. 2). And what is the consummation of the kingdom of God compared to? What is heaven compared to? It is compared to a feast. It is compared to a great celebration (Matt. 8:11).

What Jacob sees from a prophetic distance is the messianic Son of David, the Savior who is worshiped and adored, who conquers all of his and our enemies, and who ushers in an everlasting period of peace.[7] The result is the praise of his people as the tribute of nations comes to him who rules forever. His kingdom can never be conquered and there can be no end of the abundance of good things: joy, peace, and celebration. This king from the tribe of Judah will come from David's own body.

David is a type of the final, heavenly (eschatological) fulfillment. David is from the tribe of Judah. He defeated the Jebusites and took possession of Zion (2 Sam. 5:6-7); he "became greater and greater for the Lord the God of hosts was with him" (2 Sam. 5:10), and the Lord gave him "rest from all his surrounding enemies" (2 Sam. 7:1).

David's offspring, Solomon, also foreshadows the peace and prosperity that comes through the righteous rule of Jesus. The rule of Solomon is described in idyllic terms:

> [20] Judah and Israel were as many as the sand by the sea. They ate and drank and were happy. [21] Solomon ruled over all the kingdoms from the Euphrates to the land of the Philistines and to the border of Egypt. They brought tribute and served Solomon all the days of his life. [22] Solomon's provision for one day was thirty cors of fine flour and sixty cors of meal, [23] ten fat oxen, and twenty pasture-fed cattle, a hundred sheep, besides deer, gazelles, roebucks, and fattened fowl. [24] For he had dominion over all the region west of the Euphrates from Tiphsah to Gaza, over all the kings west of the Euphrates. And he had peace on all sides around him. [25] And Judah and Israel lived in safety, from Dan even to Beersheba, every man under his vine and under his fig tree, all the days of Solomon. (1 Ki. 4:20-25)

Without question, the gracious covenant with David, extended through Solomon, is an expansion of the covenant of grace promised to Adam after his transgression and carried on through the patriarch Abraham. Paul Williamson summarizes:

---

[7] How doth Christ execute the office of a king? A. Christ executeth the office of a king, in subduing us to himself, in ruling and defending us, and in restraining and conquering all his and our enemies. (Westminster Shorter Catechism Q/A 26). Jesus is "…our eternal king who governs us by his Word and Spirit, and who guards us and keeps us in the freedom he has won for us." (Heidelberg Catechism Lord's Day 12, Q/A 31)

...both Abraham and David are promised 'a great name' (Gen. 12:2; 2 Sam. 7:9); victory over enemies (Gen. 22:17; 2 Sam. 7:11 cf. Ps. 89:23); a special divine-human relationship (Gen. 17:7-8; 2 Sam. 7:24; cf. Ps. 89:26), and a special line of 'seed' through which their name would be perpetuated (Gen. 21:12; 2 Sam. 7:14; cf. Pss. 89:30-32; 132:12), and a unique descendant of both would mediate international blessing (Gen. 22:18; ps. 72:17).[8]

While God calls David "my servant,"[9] he calls David's offspring "my son" (2 Sam. 7:14). Sonship, in relation to God, is relatively rare in the Old Testament. Israel is called God's son (Ex. 4:22-23) and Adam's sonship is confirmed by the New Testament (cf. Gen. 5:1-3 with Luke 3:38). David's son will also be God's Son in a special, howbeit qualified, sense. Robertson writes:

> The prospect of chastening of the 'son of God' (II Sam. 7:14b) spoils any effort to find the "divine kingship" concept of the Ancient Near East manifested in Israel's understand of its monarchy. Yet at the same time, the declaration of II Samuel 7:14 that David's son also is God's Son provides adequate basis for latter developments which point toward a 'divine Messiah.'[10]

The moral and spiritual failure of Judah's kings met with God's displeasure and discipline. The succession of kings ended in exile. But as the Israelites returned to the Promised Land, this promise would certainly be remembered. One from David's own body would come, bringing with him an even greater kingdom. When the royal, divine Son comes from David's own body (Rom. 1:3), he will have a royal task to perform.

God's house

Once the Jebusites had been conquered and the ark of the covenant brought to Jerusalem, David's thoughts turn toward a temple to house the ark. David's desire was to build the heavenly king an earthly palace. Both tabernacle and temple were earthly copies of God's heavenly palace. Because God's throne was brought to Jerusalem and because God's kingship is so much greater than any earthly monarch, it seemed only natural to begin the building process. But God told David, "No."

---

[8] Paul R. Williamson, *Sealed with an Oath*, New Studies in Biblical Theology (Downers Grove: Apollos/IVP; 2007), 144.

[9] Before David, only Abraham (Gen. 26:24), Moses (Num. 12:7) and Caleb (Num. 14:24) were called "my servant."

[10] Robertson, *Christ of the Covenants*, 234.

David wanted to do something good for the Lord. He wanted to honor God and exalt him above all the gods of the nations. He was willing to undertake the task, but God refused his wishes. I would think that this would be incredibly discouraging. We go throughout life learning this sometimes difficult lesson that God's "no" is always for our good. David wanted to build God a royal house. God, in turn, declares that he will build a house for David. He will establish a royal dynasty for David.[11]

The astounding grace of God is summarily captured in all of his "I" statements:

> [8] Now, therefore, thus you shall say to my servant David, 'Thus says the Lord of hosts, *I took you* from the pasture, from following the sheep, that you should be prince over my people Israel. [9] And *I have been with you* wherever you went and have cut off all your enemies from before you. And *I will make for you a great name,* like the name of the great ones of the earth. [10] And *I will appoint a place for my people Israel* and will plant them, so that they may dwell in their own place and be disturbed no more. And violent men shall afflict them no more, as formerly, [11]... And *I will give you rest* from all your enemies. Moreover, the Lord declares to you that *the Lord will make you a house.* [12] When your days are fulfilled and you lie down with your fathers, *I will raise up your offspring* after you, who shall come from your body, and *I will establish his kingdom.* [13] He shall build a house for my name, and *I will establish the throne* of his kingdom forever. [14] *I will be to him a father*, and he shall be to me a son. (2 Sam. 7:8-14, emphasis mine)

God's great and gracious promises continue to expand as redemptive history unfolds. God had already planted Israel in the Promised Land, and yet the Lord speaks of appointing a place for his people (7:10). God had already given David rest from all his surrounding enemies (7:1), but in this covenant the Lord promises him rest from all his enemies (7:11). David already has offspring (1 Chron. 3:4), but God promises him an offspring (7:11-12). David's kingdom will be transferred to Solomon (cf.

---

[11] The reference to David's house is not to a physical building, but a dynasty. David's house is correlated with David's offspring (2 Sam. 7:12). That David understood it this way is also clear from 2 Samuel 7:18, "Then King David went in and sat before the Lord and said, "Who am I, O Lord God, and what is my house, that you have brought me thus far?"" Cf. vv. 19, 25-26. Throughout 2 Samuel 7 there is a play on words. The Hebrew word for David's house, God's house and David's dynasty is the same, *bayît*.

1 Ki. 2:12), but God promised that his son's throne would be non-transferable (7:13). Clearly, God is promising something that transcends Jerusalem and her kings. These are physical, spiritual, and eternal blessings. What God *wills* transcends what Solomon and the kings after him enjoyed while on earth.

God's will for his people is always for their good. But how often do we find ourselves less than thrilled about God's will and ways? Rather than conforming our wills to his, we find ourselves uncomfortably in the place of Romans 7, "For what I will to do, that I do not practice; but what I hate, that I do. For the good that I will to do, I do not do; but the evil I will not to do that I practice" (Rom. 7:15, 19 NKJV). Fortunately that is not the final "I will" statement of the Bible. The Lord graciously declares, "*I will* put my laws in their mind and write them on their hearts; and *I will* be their God, and they shall be My people… For *I will* be merciful toward their iniquities and *I will* remember their sins no more" (Heb. 8:10, 12; emphasis mine).

Redemptive history begins with God declaring, "I will put enmity between you and the woman, between your offspring and her offspring…" (Gen. 3:15) and in the final book of the Bible the Lord declares, "To him who overcomes I will give to eat from the Tree of Life" (Rev. 2:7). "I will give you the crown of life" (Rev. 2:10). "I will give of the fountain of the water of life freely to him who thirsts" (Rev. 21:6). He will do these things through David's royal Son Jesus.

In this covenant relationship, God promises to establish David's house and in turn, David's royal son will build a house for the Lord. Solomon will build the temple. As we saw in chapter 2, the temple that Solomon built was reminiscent of God's sanctuary in the Garden of Eden. Returning to God's house was always the hope of God's people. Though the temple builders of Babel wanted a tower to reach into the heavens (Gen. 11:1-9), God showed Jacob a ladder where heaven and earth met (Gen. 28:12). Though Egypt had their impressive temples, the Lord will only be found in the place he has chosen to put his name, which would be committed to Solomon to carry out.

But what man could build such a temple? Solomon recognized the impossibility of this task in his prayer of dedication. "But will God indeed dwell on the earth? Behold, heaven and the highest heaven cannot contain you; how much less this house that I have built!" (1 Ki. 8:27). The Lord rules from his temple. From it the law of God went forth (Isa. 2:3). To this place Gentiles would come (1 Ki. 8:41-43; 10:1-13). The temple was the place of rejoicing (Pss. 42:1-4; 122:1-9; 137:6). This is the place where prayers, like incense, rise, and sacrificial animals are slain. This is the place where the fate of the nations rests (Amos 1:1-15), and the final destiny of the world depends upon this God who has chosen Mount Zion to dwell (Isa. 2:2-4; Mic. 4:1-3). Bruce Waltke observes:

> This one place of worship reinforces the truth that there is only one God, not many, and avoids Israel's temptation to serve other gods, for many high places may tempt the unwary (Deut. 12:1-9; Judg. 10:6). The temple's architectural features contain both cosmological and royal symbols that teach *I AM's* [God's] absolute sovereignty over the whole creation and his special headship over Israel.[12]

With the construction of the temple complete, the ark of the covenant was brought into the temple (1 Ki. 8:1). The priests took it into the Most Holy Place, underneath the wings of the cherubim (1 Ki. 8:6ff.). The ark of the covenant with the cherubim was built for the enthronement of God (Ex. 25:10-22; 29:42-46; Num. 7:89; 1 Sam. 4:4). As the people watched the priests enter and exit, the Lord of glory graced his people with the sign of his eternal presence:

> And when the priests came out of the Holy Place, a cloud filled the house of the Lord, so that the priests could not stand to minister because of the cloud, for the glory of the Lord filled the house of the Lord." (1 Ki. 8:10-11; cf. Ex. 40:34-35)

The Lord of the covenant is faithful to his promises. He raised up an offspring for David, and David's offspring built a temple for the King of Majesty. The third element of this covenant relationship has to do with the throne of David.

Throne

"And your house and your kingdom shall be made sure forever before me. Your throne shall be established forever" (2 Sam. 7:16).

The Lord promised David an eternal throne. Obviously an eternal throne is something that, properly speaking, belongs to God alone. But at the coronation of David's son, we see the close connection between God's throne and the throne of David. On the top of Mount Zion the throne of David and Yahweh coalesce:

> [22] And they ate and drank before the Lord on that day with great gladness. And they made Solomon the son of David king the second time, and they anointed him as prince for the Lord, and Zadok as priest. [23] Then Solomon sat on the throne of the

---

[12] Bruce Waltke, *An Old Testament Theology* (Grand Rapids: Zondervan, 2007), 709.

> Lord as king in place of David his father. And he prospered, and all Israel obeyed him. (1 Chron. 29:22-23)

If it wasn't in sacred Scripture, we might not believe it. The author of 1 Chronicles said that "Solomon sat upon the throne of the Lord." On one level, the Lord had seated his anointed upon his glorious throne. But again, we must say that this perspective points us beyond Solomon to the one who is worthy to sit upon God's throne and rule forever. The enthronement of Solomon called upon Israel not to rest contented in this moment, but to look to the future, to look for the truly righteous king who delivers his offspring from all their enemies, the one who gathers them around the eternal throne of God where he himself sits. This covenant with David teaches us that the one who is able to do these things will be a man who has both the heart of God and the heart of man.

As the history of Israel goes, Solomon's heart did not remain true. Though he is called God's son (2 Sam. 7:14), he must experience the chastening of the Lord. While we have stressed the gracious promises of God's covenant with David, there are also consequences for refusing to reign under the authority of God's rule. The Lord promised to discipline the Son of David with the rod and with the stripes of man (2 Sam. 7:14).

As the king gave his final instructions to his son, he emphasized the covenant loyalty required of the newly crowned king. David said:

> ² "I am about to go the way of all the earth. Be strong, and show yourself a man, ³ and keep the charge of the Lord your God, walking in his ways and keeping his statutes, his commandments, his rules, and his testimonies, as it is written in the Law of Moses, that you may prosper in all that you do and wherever you turn, ⁴ *that* the Lord may establish his word that he spoke concerning me, saying, '*If* your sons pay close attention to their way, to walk before me in faithfulness with all their heart and with all their soul, you shall not lack a man on the throne of Israel.' (1 Ki. 2:2-4, emphasis mine)

The Lord appeared to Solomon and reiterated these words in the form of a warning:

> ⁶ But if you turn aside from following me, you or your children, and do not keep my commandments and my statutes that I have set before you, but go and serve other gods and worship them, ⁷ then I will cut off Israel from the land that I have given them, and the house that I have consecrated for my name I will cast out of my sight, and Israel will become a proverb and a byword among all peoples. (1 Ki. 9:6-7)

The echoes of Eden return once more. If Solomon fails to obey, the people will perish away from the land. Keeping the commandments of

God was the stipulation for life in the Promised Land, not only for the royal crown but also the common people. But it is just like the heart of man to challenge God's rule. Solomon's wives turned his heart to follow after the gods of the nations that the Lord had driven out (1 Ki. 11:4-8). As the Mosaic covenant made clear, the price to be paid for rebellion was very costly. The curses of the covenant fell upon the nation that had sworn to do all that God commanded. The Lord was angry; he tore the kingdom from David's son and gave all but one tribe to Solomon's servant (1 Ki. 11:9-13). This was the beginning of the end and given all that we have looked at, it creates a certain amount of tension. How could this be an everlasting covenant with David?

The covenant with David was and is about Christ

As we saw in the Abrahamic covenant, there are two levels of fulfillment. God promised to give Abraham an offspring. Abraham's descendants become as numerous as the sand of the sea. God swore an oath that he would give his descendants the Promised Land, and so he did. But there is another level, a deeper level. Paul looked at the promise of the offspring, and in Galatians 3:16 he said that the promise was not "referring to many, but referring to one, 'And to your offspring,' who is Christ."

It worked the same way for the land. God swore to give Israel the land and when Israel entered Canaan after their forty years of wilderness wandering, the promise was fulfilled on one level. "Not one word has failed of all the good things that the Lord your God promised concerning you. All have come to pass for you; not one of them has failed" (Josh. 23:14). Yet the writer of Hebrews tells us that there is a second, deeper level to the Abrahamic promise. "For he [Abraham] was looking forward to the city that has foundations, whose designer and builder is God" (Heb. 11:10-16).

If Christ is the ultimate reality of the Abrahamic covenant, and if the Davidic covenant is an extension and expansion of the Abrahamic covenant, then we must conclude that the promises to David are about Christ and His kingdom. And this is exactly how the writers of the New Testament understood it:

> [1] Paul, a servant of Christ Jesus, called to be an apostle, set apart for the gospel of God, [2] which he promised beforehand through his prophets in the holy Scriptures, [3] concerning his Son, *who was descended from David according to the flesh* [4] and was declared to be the Son of God in power according to the Spirit of holiness by his resurrection from the dead, Jesus Christ our Lord. (Rom. 1:1-4, emphasis mine)

He is David's son according to the flesh but is greater than David because he is declared to be the Son of God in power. How? By his resurrection from the dead (v. 4). This is the answer to the dilemma of the Davidic covenant. As Dennis Johnson underscores:

> These intolerable tensions arise from the fact that life and blessing in covenant communion with God is, on the one hand, *absolutely secured* by God's promise, and yet it is, on the other, certainly *contingent* on the submissive obedience of God's servant-people and their leaders. How, indeed, can God's richest, greatest promises come true for his people, if those blessings are to any degree contingent on the faithful obedience of the human covenant servant (whether Israel/Judah or the king)? As the books of Samuel-Kings show so clearly, sons of David who resemble their ancestor in whole-souled commitment were few and far between. Worse yet, as 2 Samuel demonstrates too clearly, David himself was far from a perfect prototype of just and holy leadership. The "man after God's heart" (Acts 13:22) also abused his power and position to gratify his desires, cover his guilt, and exploit his loyal subjects. In order for the richest blessing promised by the Lord to come to his people, we needed the arrival of a covenant Servant characterized by a purity of devotion to God unparalleled by anyone in Israel's previous history... the unresolved tensions within the Old Testament cried out for resolution in the coming of the Lord and the coming of a Servant unstained by the infidelities that had always polluted Israel and her leaders.[13]

He is called the Son of God (2 Sam. 7:14; Mk. 15:39). Unlike David, no iniquity was found in Jesus (Jn. 19:4), and yet the stripes of man were laid upon him (2 Sam. 7:14; Isa. 53:5-6). He walked before God with integrity of heart and uprightness of life, doing all that God commanded him and keeping the Lord's statutes and rules (1 Ki. 9:5). Nevertheless Jesus experienced the curse of the covenant upon the cross and was cut off from the land of the living (1 Ki. 9:7; Gal. 3:13; Matt. 27:45-46).

And we would say that this is *not* how it is supposed to end. He should have been given the throne in Jerusalem, not a cross on Calvary. When does Jesus sit upon David's throne? Some are still waiting for that day, but the writers of the New Testament saw that day and proclaimed that it had been fulfilled:

---

[13] Dennis E. Johnson, *Him We Proclaim: Preaching Christ from All the Scriptures* (Philipsburg, NJ: Presbyterian and Reformed, 2007), 230.

> ³² And we bring you the good news that what God promised to the fathers, ³³ this he has fulfilled to us their children by raising Jesus, as also it is written in the second Psalm, "'You are my Son, today I have begotten you.' ³⁴ And as for the fact that he raised him from the dead, no more to return to corruption, he has spoken in this way, "'I will give you the holy and sure blessings of David.' ³⁵ Therefore he says also in another psalm, "'You will not let your Holy One see corruption.' ³⁶ For David, after he had served the purpose of God in his own generation, fell asleep and was laid with his fathers and saw corruption, ³⁷ but he whom God raised up did not see corruption. (Acts 13:32-37)

Paul was quoting from the second psalm of David. It is a psalm of the ascension of the king's son to the throne. At the resurrection Christ is given the holy and sure blessings of David. There he will see no corruption. His throne is secure forever. His kingdom will not come to an end because he rules over his kingdom by the power of his everlasting life (Heb. 7:14-16).

Likewise, the apostle Peter did not understand the promises of this covenant as ultimately referring to a succession of sons that would lead to the Messiah finally taking his place upon the throne of David *in* Jerusalem. He did not see this covenant fulfilled in a millennial reign of Christ *from* Jerusalem. The covenant with David is fulfilled at the resurrection and ascension of Christ when he assumed the seat of David forever. No earthly throne will do, for he is the king who is truly man *and* truly God:

> ²⁹Brothers, I may say to you with confidence about the patriarch David that he both died and was buried, and his tomb is with us to this day. ³⁰ Being therefore a prophet, and knowing that God had sworn with an oath to him that he would set one of his descendants on his throne, ³¹ he foresaw and spoke about the resurrection of the Christ, that he was not abandoned to Hades, nor did his flesh see corruption. ³² This Jesus God raised up, and of that we all are witnesses. ³³ Being therefore exalted at the right hand of God, and having received from the Father the promise of the Holy Spirit, he has poured out this that you yourselves are seeing and hearing. ³⁴ For David did not ascend into the heavens, but he himself says,
>
> "'The Lord said to my Lord,
>
> "Sit at my right hand,
>
> ³⁵ until I make your enemies your footstool.'"

³⁶ Let all the house of Israel therefore know for certain that God has made him both Lord and Christ, this Jesus whom you crucified. (Acts 2:29-36)

When Christ ascended on high and was seated at God's right hand, what did he do? He poured out his Holy Spirit upon the church, *the temple of the living God*. Here is the incredible reality of the Davidic covenant. David's son is building a house for God's name, not with wood and precious stones, but with living stones. The church is the temple of God:

> ¹⁹ Now, therefore, you are no longer strangers and foreigners, but fellow citizens with the saints and members of the household of God, ²⁰ having been built on the foundation of the apostles and prophets, Jesus Christ Himself being the chief cornerstone, ²¹ in whom the whole building, being joined together, grows into a holy temple in the Lord, ²² in whom you also are being built together for a dwelling place of God in the Spirit. (Eph. 2:9-22)

The progress of God's covenants

God gave to Adam a covenant of works, and Adam failed. Jesus underwent the covenant of works and succeeded. In the covenant of grace, God promised that an offspring would come in bruised victory. Jesus fulfills Adam's commission by filling the earth with the glory of God as he creates an ever-growing place for God's name, from one end of the earth to the other. Like righteous Noah, Jesus is God's righteous Son who spares his children by doing all that God commanded him. Out of every tribe, tongue, and language Jesus is the one who breathes life into spiritually dead people, making them the offspring of Abraham and bringing them into the Promised Land. By his active obedience he fulfills the law's demands, and by his passive obedience he walks the path of blood alone, taking upon himself the penalty for his people's covenant breaking. This king has the power to set Abraham's captive offspring free. And even now, as we journey toward the new heavens and earth, we do so under the protection of our righteous king Jesus, who ascended to heaven to show that he is head of his church and that the Father rules all things through him.¹⁴ When the end comes, we will experience the joy of the new heavens and earth. The throne of God will descend, and we will see this king, David's king, seated upon the throne of the Lord in the midst of the garden of God, worshiped for all eternity by his royal subjects.

---

¹⁴ Heidelberg Catechism Lord's Day 19, Q/A 50.

> When we've been there ten thousand years,
> Bright shining as the sun,
> We've no less days to sing God's praise
> Than when we've first begun.[15]

Study Questions:

1. What is the significance of the ark of the covenant and its relocation to Jerusalem?
2. What did the Lord promise David in this covenant?
3. How do the promises of the Davidic covenant further the covenant of grace?
4. How can this covenant with David be eternal since the line of enthroned kings was broken and the temple destroyed?
5. What can we learn about Jesus in the Davidic covenant?

---

[15] John Newton, "Amazing Grace" (1790).

Chapter 7: The New Covenant: A Reason to Rejoice

> God calls us to himself without effect as long as he speaks to us in no other way than by the voice of man.[1]

A fractured existence

Shortly after King Solomon's death the kingdom of Israel splits in two. The ten northern tribes follow Jeroboam, but the tribe of Benjamin remains loyal to the king of Judah. The northern kingdom slides into apostasy and is finally taken into captivity when the Assyrians overrun the land. The tribes of the north, who were direct descendants of Abraham, circumcised with the circumcision made with hands, become as it were, "uncircumcised" and are expelled from the land. The northern kingdom undergoes the curses of the covenant just as Moses had warned in the Law (Deut. 27-28). Now only the southern kingdom remained in the land promised to Abraham, Isaac, and Jacob.

Judah's decline

Like the tribes of the north, so also the southern tribes violate the covenant made at Sinai. Despite the occasional reforms of good kings, Judah turns from God and proves to be faithless to their word. Because God is never unfaithful, having repeatedly warned of the consequences for violating the covenant, the Lord unleashes the covenant curses upon the southern kingdom. Because the Promised Land returns to the shrouded darkness of pagan worship, even the light of the temple is put out.

    The high point in the book of Kings is the building of God's temple. It is a project that mirrors the week of creation taking seven years to complete. Like in the time of Noah, the rebellion during the time of the kings leads to de-creation. Little by little the house of God is dismantled, and the treasures are taken away. In a bitter twist of divine irony, the first

---

[1] John Calvin, *Commentaries on the Epistle of Paul the Apostle to the Hebrews* (Grand Rapids: Baker, 1999), 188-189.

foreign king to plunder the temple of the Lord and take away its goods is the king of Egypt (2 Chron. 12:9). Israel plundered the Egyptians before leaving Egypt, and from the spoil the furnishings for the tabernacle were likely made. The Egyptians are the first to come up to the temple and reclaim their gold (1 Ki. 14:25-26).

The kings of Syria take their turns at plundering the temple (1 Ki. 15:18; 2 Ki. 12:18). Even the northern king of Israel "seized all the gold and silver and all the vessels that were found in the house of the Lord along with the treasuries of the king's house" (2 Ki. 14:14). The last foreign king to plunder the house of the Lord is Nebuchadnezzar, the king of Babylon (2 Ki. 24:13). He razed it to the ground.

This final invasion by the king of Babylon is precipitated by the wickedness of King Manasseh. This king commits child sacrifice, and he places statues of pagan deities in the temple of the Lord. He also consults mediums and necromancers. As the saying goes, Manassah "did it all" (2 Ki. 21:4-7).

Judah does have eight good kings after David and Solomon. Reforms take place. Judah also has twelve wicked kings. The Lord brings the twelve tribes out of Egypt and into the Promised Land, but in that Promised Land twelve wicked kings of Judah would reign. When the twelfth king of Judah goes astray, the wrath of God is filled up, and the Davidic era comes to an end.

With the curse being carried out, the question is: would there be blessing in Israel's future? That is largely the theme of Jeremiah 31. When it looks to be the darkest hour for Israel, God announces that there will be light again for the sake of his covenant promises. A new covenant will not only be made, it will be kept.

The new covenant

What is the new covenant about? The new covenant will be different from the old covenant made at Sinai. Unlike that covenant, the new will not be broken. God's Son will be perfectly faithful to his heavenly Father. And in this new covenant that Christ brings comes a greater knowledge of God, the law written upon the hearts, along with the securing of complete and irrevocable forgiveness of sins.

How the new covenant connects to the previous covenants
As only God could drive out the nations that would tempt Israel to sin, only God can drive out the desires of the heart to sin against him. A new covenant is needed, and a better covenant is Israel's only hope. There is a great need for a righteous king who will rule righteously. There is also a need for an enduring temple to be built in a kingdom that would have no

end. The failure of the people to do as God commanded them through Moses needs to be remedied if any of Abraham's offspring would be spared. God promised to hold his hand back from destroying the world with a flood, but Israel was overrun by foreign armies and swept away. Is there an ark of salvation? Is there a righteous deliverer who can bring them back from the judgment? Has the serpent succeeded? Has the poison of his venom worked through the entire line of Adam?

The promises of the covenant of grace would not be thwarted. Adam will have a faithful offspring (Gen. 3:15) who will lead his people into the eternal Garden of Eden. He will bring them safely through the waters, (Gen. 7-8; 1 Pet. 3:20-21) even though he walks through the severed animals alone (Gen. 15; Jn. 13:36). All that the Lord commands him, he will do (Ex. 24:7). He will execute justice and mercy as the obedient king and will build the temple of the Lord (1 Cor. 3:16-17).

This new covenant with its complete forgiveness of sins and transformation of the people of God will not be broken. God is not only going to rescue his people from the serpent and from his own wrath, he is going to definitively deal with their sins and change their hearts. The new covenant promises what only Christ can fulfill.

Who is God making this covenant with?

> [31]Behold, the days are coming, declares the Lord, when I will make a new covenant with the house of Israel and the house of Judah... [33] For this is the covenant that I will make with the house of Israel after those days. (Jer. 31:31, 33)

The new covenant will be made with the house of Israel and Judah, which is to say, Abraham's children. As the Bible makes abundantly clear, blood-born descent does not secure a lasting status in Abraham's family; only faith laying hold of Abraham's Savior, Jesus Christ, brings a person into the family of promise, the family of God. Not only the northern tribes but also believing Gentiles would be members of this covenant (Gal. 3:16, 26-29; 2 Cor. 3:6; Eph. 2:12-18).[2] What will the covenant be like? It is stated in the negative.

Not like the old covenant
This new covenant is:

---

[2] With the northern kingdom being thoroughly assimilated into the cultures where the Assyrians had placed them, we could speak of the 10 Tribes as becoming Gentiles. Certainly the Jews would consider them such if the Samaritans are any indicator.

> not like the covenant that I made with their fathers on the day when I took them by the hand to bring them out of the land of Egypt, my covenant that they broke, though I was their husband, declares the Lord. (Jer. 31:32)

While there are certainly themes common to both the Mosaic covenant and the new covenant, the emphasis appears to be upon the differences between the two.[3] Yahweh said that this covenant is *not* going to be like the one God made with Israel at Mt. Sinai. Here is the great contrast, *it will not be another law covenant*. It will not be another covenant where the blessings enjoyed in the land or curses that remove the people from the land are contingent upon their obedience or disobedience to the terms of the covenant. Again, there is grace undergirding the Mosaic covenant even as there is a works principle running through it, calling out to the Israelites, "Do this law and live" (Deut. 29:9; Lev. 18:5). This covenant had to come to an end (Heb. 8:6-8, 13) because there was a double insufficiency: one having to do with the inability of the law (Rom. 8:3) and the other with the inability of those under the law. Calvin writes:

> Though the crime of violating the covenant was justly imputed to the people, who had through their own perfidy [deceitfulness] departed from God, yet the weakness of the covenant is also pointed out, because it was not written in their hearts.[4]

A new covenant is required because Israel's unfaithfulness ended in the same dead-end cul-de-sac of judgment and exile. They were held to their blood-sworn oath, and so the psalmist lamented, "They have poured

---

[3] The new covenant does not come in and completely obliterate everything in the old covenant. If it did, we would have no reason for seeing the 10 Commandments as a guide for showing gratitude to God for our salvation. There is also continuity in that both old covenant and new covenant believers are saved by grace, through faith in Christ. old covenant believers looked for the coming of the Messiah, and we, as new covenant believers, look back in faith to the saving work of our Messiah. Yet the differences between the two cannot be swept aside. As Peterson has pointed out, even "...the expression 'Behold the days are coming,' introduces the note of change (vv. 27, 31 and 38)." David G. Peterson, *Transformed by God: new covenant Life and Ministry* (Downers Grove: Intervaristy, 2012), 29.

[4] John Calvin, *Commentaries on the Epistle of Paul the Apostle to the Hebrews*, 186.

out their blood like water all around Jerusalem, and there was no one to bury them" (Psalm 79:3). A moat of blood surrounded Jerusalem[5] and as predicted, Israel was expelled from the land (Deut. 28:36, 63-68) because of their unfaithfulness to the Lord.

Israel's relationship to the Lord was like that of a wife to her husband. Thus says the Lord, "I remember the devotion of your youth, your love as a bride, how you followed me in the wilderness, in a land not sown" (Jer. 2:2). Israel met the Lord at Mt Sinai and made vows to be faithful to him, but the nation did not keep their wedding vows. "For long ago I broke your yoke and burst your bonds; but you said, 'I will not serve.' Yes, on every high hill and under every green tree you bowed down like a whore" (Jer. 2:20). They turned from their husband and committed spiritual adultery with the gods of the nations. God's unfaithful wife went further still:

> [23] How can you say, 'I am not unclean, I have not gone after the Baals'? Look at your way in the valley; know what you have done— a restless young camel running here and there, [24] a wild donkey used to the wilderness, in her heat sniffing the wind! Who can restrain her lust? None who seek her need weary themselves; in her month they will find her. (Jer. 2:23-24)

So the Lord filed for divorce showing that that covenant relationship had been irreparably damaged. The Mosaic covenant must come to an end. Nevertheless, the grace of God would be seen as exceedingly gracious as the Lord would show his people a better way, into a better relationship, based upon better promises.

Once again the "I will" statements of the Lord show us his gracious intentions to fulfill the covenant made with Abraham even though the law appeared to threaten it (Gal. 3:17). God will make a new covenant that is *not* like the covenant with the fathers.

What is the newness of the new covenant?

1. I will put my law within them writing it upon their hearts.

2. I will be their God, and they shall be my people.

3. They will know me from the least to the greatest (differently worded, but it carries the same divine initiative).

4. I will forgive their iniquity and remember their sin no more.

---

[5] I owe this insightful observation to Rev. Matthew Barker.

As Paul Williamson rightly notes, "There is no hint here of the mutuality expressed in the Mosaic covenant. There is no conditional 'if clause' here as there clearly was back in Exodus 19:5."[6] It would be incorrect to conclude that God has no requirements for his new covenant people. The requirements are faith and repentance, and God is the one who supplies them. Gratitude of life, grounded in the gospel of Jesus Christ, will be manifested by obedience to God's word.

The important point that should be given its full weight is simply this: The new covenant, inaugurated by Christ, is never contrasted with the Abrahamic covenant. Why is that? It is because the new covenant will be the fulfillment of the promises made to Abraham and to Adam before him (Gen. 3:15).

Given Israel's wholesale abandonment of God's law, the first description of the new covenant comes as a bit of a surprise. In the new covenant the Lord does not dispense with the law (Matt. 5:17) but instead writes it upon the heart.

Law on the heart

> [33] But this is the covenant that I will make with the house of Israel after those days, declares the Lord: I will put my Law within them, and I will write it on their hearts. And I will be their God, and they shall be my people. (Jer. 31:33)

Those familiar with the law of Moses probably wouldn't have thought that this aspect of the new covenant was all that new. "You shall therefore lay up these words of mine in your heart and in your soul" (Deut. 11:18). "But the word is very near you. It is in your mouth and in your heart, so that you can do it" (Deut. 30:14).

So what's new about the new covenant? When we compare Scripture with Scripture[7], the newness is clear. In Jeremiah 17, God declares, "The sin of Judah is written with a pen of iron; with a point of diamond it is engraved on the tablet of their heart, and on the horns of their altars." (Jer. 17:1) The law of commandments, written on stone, revealed the sin of the heart. The law of the Mosaic covenant could only expose sinful hearts. It could not remove the problem; and furthermore, it could not even *change* the heart to desire to keep the law. But in the new covenant these gifts of God are given in great abundance, not to the few as in the

---

[6] Paul R. Williamson, *Sealed with an Oath*, New Studies in Biblical Theology (Downers Grove: Apollos/IVP; 2007), 153.

[7] The Reformers called this practice "the analogy of faith."

old covenant,[8] but to the many. He will circumcise the heart *"so that* you will love the Lord your God with all your heart and with all your soul, *that you may live"* (Deut 30:6; emphasis mine). This is nothing less than the new birth that Jesus spoke of in John 3.

This is the difference of the covenants. Jeremiah was sent to those whose hearts were engraved with sin. The nation stood defiantly against the law of God. But in the new covenant, God will sovereignly regenerate his people; which is to say, he will engrave the law upon their hearts so that they will obey him. Jeremiah 24:7 is a parallel new covenant passage, "I will give them a heart to know that I am the Lord, and they shall be my people and I will be their God, for they shall return to me with their whole heart."

Both John Calvin and Matthew Henry understood Jeremiah 31:33 to refer to the work of regeneration which leads to a right way of living:

> He now shews (*sic*) a difference between the Law and the Gospel, for the Gospel brings with it the grace of regeneration: its doctrine, therefore, is not that of the letter, but penetrates into the heart and reforms all the inward faculties so that obedience is rendered to the righteousness of God.[9]

> He works in them a disposition to obedience, a conformity of thought and affection to the rules of the divine Law, as that of the copy to the original. This is here promised, and ought to be prayed for, that our duty may be done conscientiously and with delight.[10]

Perhaps you are thinking to yourself, how can I be assured that I belong to the new covenant that God has made? How can I really know that the law is in my heart when I do not conform to the will of God as I should? The new covenant is not for perfect people who already have proven by their own works that they have the law of God written upon their heart. In the new covenant God's sovereign power is displayed by changing your dead heart in order to love him and to hate the sin that displeases him. The only one who obeyed God's law perfectly was the covenant mediator, Jesus Christ. Those whom God brings to Christ will seek to reform their lives according to his good word. Those who are

---

[8] Calvin called the grace of God *rare* and *little known* under the Law. Cf. John Calvin, *Commentaries on the Prophet Jeremiah and the Lamentations*; vol. 3 (Grand Rapids: Baker; 2003), 131.

[9] Calvin, *Jeremiah,* 130.

[10] Matthew Henry, *Matthew Henry's Commentary on the Whole Bible*, 6 vols. (New York: Fleming H Revel, n.d.), 4.606

given new hearts will seek to live for him and die to sin.[11] *The struggle against sin and contrary affections for God does not end in the new covenant. In this new covenant we are given the Spirit of God to wrestle not only against the world and the devil, but also the flesh* (1 Jn. 2:16). As the first aspect of the new covenant has to do with our relationship toward God, the second has to do with our relationships within the church.

The Lord will be known

> And no longer shall each one teach his neighbor and each his brother, saying, 'Know the Lord,' for they shall all know me, from the least of them to the greatest, declares the Lord.

This has been a puzzling verse for many. We are told that they will no longer have to teach their neighbor, but in the New Testament, teachers are clearly commended to the churches (Eph. 4:11-12).

Again we should expect that this prophecy addresses the historical circumstances in which Jeremiah found himself. He is told to run throughout the streets of Jerusalem and to search for people who do justice and seek truth. Jeremiah replies:

> ¹These are only the poor; they have no sense; for *they do not know the way of the Lord*, the justice of their God. ⁵ I will go to the great and will speak to them, for *they know the way of the Lord*, the justice of their God." But they all alike had broken the yoke; they had burst the bonds. (Jer. 5:1, 5; emphasis mine)

In Jeremiah's day the problem was universal, and it plagued the least to the greatest. The Israelites were in covenant with God, and yet they didn't know their Lord. The new covenant promise doesn't put a period after the words, "and they shall no longer teach his neighbor," rather it says that they shall no longer teach their neighbors to "know the Lord." In one sense we have already begun to enjoy the benefits of this new

---

[11] Since we have been delivered from our misery by God's grace alone through Christ and not because we have earned it: why then must we still do good? To be sure, Christ has redeemed us by his blood. But we do good because Christ by his Spirit is also renewing us to be like himself so that in all our living, we may show that we are thankful to God for all he has done for us, and so that he may be praised through us. And we do good so that we may be assured of our faith by its fruits, and by our godly living our neighbors may be won over to Christ. (Heidelberg Catechism Lord's Day 32, Q/A 86)

covenant promise. We still must teach others to know the Lord because there will always be tares among the wheat (Matt. 13:24-30) as well as those who have been chosen for salvation and have not yet come to faith. Believers too, need instruction in the law and the gospel of Christ to grow in Christian maturity and understanding of God. Jeremiah is not suggesting that the new covenant removes the need for instruction. What he announces is that in the new covenant, God's people will know him in a way that Israel of old failed to know him. As Jeremiah 24:7 declares:

> I will give them a heart to know me, that I am the Lord. They will be my people, and I will be their God, for they will return to me with all their heart.

The new covenant also points beyond this age to the consummation when none will have a fallen heart. Gone will be all inclinations to sin. The knowledge of God will be complete, and instruction will be needed no more. In the meantime, we never stop preaching the gospel both to the converted and to the unconverted among us. The gospel is not only necessary for conversion, it is absolutely necessary for sanctification.[12]

Jeremiah searched throughout Jerusalem for those who demonstrated that they knew the Lord by doing justice and seeking the truth, but he found none. The poor did not know the way of the Lord (Jer. 5:4). The great did not know the way of the Lord or the justice of their God (Jer. 5:5). This was the problem of the nation. The priests did not say, "'Where is the Lord?' Those who handle the law did not know me" (Jer. 2:8). God's people did not know the rules of the Lord (Jer. 8:7). "'They do not know me,' declares the Lord" (Jer. 9:3). "'They refuse to know me', declares the Lord" (Jer. 9:6). There is the pure truth; an unchanged heart *refuses* to know the Lord. But in the new covenant, when God changes the heart, his people will know him and will obey.

Jeremiah could only announce this new covenant. He could only see it from a distance as he stood day after day, calling out to the covenant people, "know the Lord, listen to his voice, defend the cause of the poor, and execute justice and mercy and righteousness." But from the least to the greatest, the people refused to listen. God said those days will be reversed when I make a new covenant with the people. What is the hinge upon which this new covenant turns?

---

[12] The Westminster Shorter Catechism describes sanctification as "the work of God's free grace, whereby we are renewed in the whole man after the image of God, and are enabled more and more to die unto sin, and live unto righteousness." (WSC 35)

Abounding grace

> For I will forgive their iniquity, and I will remember their sin no more. (Jer. 31:34)

The knowledge of sin could not be easily avoided in the old covenant. In fact, the law was not added to give grace; it was added because of transgression (Gal. 3:18-19); it was added because "sin is not counted where there is no law" (Rom. 5:13). The weakness of the Mosaic covenant was in its inability to remove sin (Heb. 7:18; 10:4). The annual sacrifices were reminders that sin could never be atoned for in this way (Heb. 10:3). People were not forgiven by offering the right sacrificial animal or by receiving absolution from the priest. God's people past, present, and future are only forgiven as they look with faith to the one to whom the sacrifices and the priesthood pointed (Pss. 51:1-9; 110).

When God remembers sins, he judges: "Now he will remember their iniquity and punish their sins" (Jer. 14:10). In the new covenant the Lord promises to "remember their sin no more." He will not judge them for their sins because their sins will be judged in a righteous substitute (Isa. 53).

From the kings of Judah to the peasants in the street, Israel had collectively left the Lord in pursuit of false gods. The heart of the people was only sin, and God remembered and judged. The temple was removed. The earthly throne of David was thrown down, but that is only half the story. The massive turning point in redemptive history would come. It would turn death to life, lawlessness to obedience, ignorance to knowledge, and condemnation to pardon. When the great High Priest came, he brought with him irreversible change.

Christ of the new covenant

The author of Hebrews tells us that there has been a change in priesthood (Heb. 7-10). Christ Jesus is priest according to the order of Melchizedek, without beginning and end (Heb. 7). This makes Jesus the guarantee of a better covenant (Heb. 7:22; 9:11). When there is a change in priesthood, there is necessarily a change in the law (Heb. 7:12). Likewise the old covenant came to an end when Jesus put the new covenant into effect by his death (Heb. 9:15-16). His death is a sacrifice "that redeems them from the transgressions committed under the first covenant" (Heb. 9:15; first covenant = Mosaic covenant). His blood sprinkles guilty consciences clean (Heb. 9:13-14; 10:22). By his single sacrifice, he has perfected his people forever (Heb. 10:14). As mediator of the new covenant for his people, they know the Lord through him and draw close to God through the heavenly curtain (Heb. 10:19-25).

The author of Hebrews makes three crucial statements about the unrivaled glories of the new covenant that Jesus brings:
1. But when Christ had offered for all time a single sacrifice for sins, he sat down at the right hand of God (Heb. 10:12).
2. But as it is, Christ has obtained a ministry that is as much more excellent than the old as the covenant he mediates is better, since it is enacted on better promises (Heb. 8:6).
3. In speaking of a new covenant, he makes the first one obsolete. And what is becoming obsolete and growing old is ready to vanish away (Heb. 8:13).

There can be no loitering in the shadows of the Old Testament now that the one to whom they testified has come. He is seated victoriously and provides a better covenant for his people. Like John the Baptist, who must decrease as Christ increases, so also the old covenant serves its purpose and passes away. These promises and present realities of the new covenant also point forward to the new heavens and earth where we will be filled with a perfected knowledge. Therefore our hearts will no longer be locked in a struggle between obedience and its opposite as we live in a place where sins and our constant covenant breaking will be things of the past and remembered no more.

In the covenants of the Bible, we find that only Jesus can satisfy the longings of God's covenant people. Adam and Eve looked for an offspring to crush the serpent. Noah looked for a righteous Savior to save and preserve him from the wrath of God. Abraham and his descendants looked for the offspring who would multiply them and bring them into their eternal inheritance. Moses looked for the truly righteous and holy Son of Israel. David looked for a king whose kingdom would have no end, and Jeremiah spoke of Christ, who would keep the covenant of works so that the covenant of grace with all of its new covenant promises would be ours.

Conclusion

Taking in the realities of this covenant, we could contrast the benefits we enjoy in the following ways:
1. The old covenant could be broken. The new covenant can never be broken.
2. The old covenant could only serve as a reminder of sin. In the new covenant, sin is atoned for.
3. The old covenant was filled with the blood of bulls and goats. The new covenant has one Lamb of God, sacrificed once for the sins of his people.
4. The old covenant was temporary. The new covenant is eternal.

5. The old covenant had many prophets, priests, and kings. The new covenant has one prophet, priest, and king.
6. The old covenant was a writing of the law on stone. The new covenant is the law written on human hearts.
7. The old covenant was a shadow of Christ. The new covenant is the reality of Christ.

Old Covenant	New Covenant
The old covenant could be broken.	The new covenant can never be broken.
The old covenant could only serve as a reminder of sin.	In the new covenant sin is atoned for.
The old covenant was filled with the blood of bulls and goats.	The new covenant has one Lamb of God, sacrificed once for the sins of his people.
The old covenant was temporary.	The new covenant is eternal.
The old covenant had many prophets, priests, and kings,	The new covenant has one prophet, priest, and king,
The old covenant was a writing of the law on stone.	The new covenant is the law written on human hearts.
The old covenant casts a shadow of Christ.	The new covenant is the reality of Christ.

Study Questions:

1. Why was the new covenant necessary?
2. How does the new covenant expand the covenant of grace?
3. How will the new covenant be like/not like the old covenant with Israel?
4. What does the new covenant teach us about the eternal state?
5. How does the new covenant show us Christ?

Chapter 8: The Covenant Servant: Promises Kept

> Long before he sent his Son to bring rescue in "the fullness of time: (Gal. 4:4), he sovereignly designed events, institutions, and individual leaders to provide foretastes of the feast, whetting Israel's appetite for the coming Savior and salvation. Israel's historical experience of blessing and judgment, weal and woe, also prepared a rich symbolic "vocabulary," embedded in the dust and blood of real history: concepts and categories pre-designed to articulate the sufficiency and complexity of Jesus' saving work.[1]

Things new and old

If we have learned nothing else from the covenants, and I do indeed hope you have learned more, we ought to be convinced that God's plan to save his people through Jesus Christ unfolds through the successive covenants of the Bible. The sovereign Lord, who decrees salvation, determines the way in which salvation is going to be achieved. The covenants of the Bible find their fulfillment in the agent of God's salvation, God's Son. In this chapter, I will explore another facet of this truth. Because Jesus is the second Adam (Rom. 5:14), the faithful Son of Abraham (Matt. 1:1), we might expect that Jesus brings in the new, but he does so in ways that were anticipated in the Old Testament.

As we cross the bridge from the Old to the New Testament, we will do three things. First, we will look at the evidence of the New Testament for finding Christ in the Old Testament. Second, we are going to take a stroll through one of the key moments in Old Testament history, namely the Exodus. We will have to be somewhat selective here, hitting the high points in the story of how God broke the bondage of his people in slavery to the Egyptians, entered into a covenant with them, and brought them

---

[1] Dennis E. Johnson, *Him We Proclaim: Preaching Christ from All the Scriptures* (Philipsburg, NJ: Presbyterian and Reformed, 2007), 198-199.

into the Promised Land. Third, we will look at the storyline of the Gospel of Matthew to see how Jesus retraces these steps of Israel.

Covenants are about Christ because the Bible is about Christ

There are many themes in the Bible: covenant, creation, kingdom, salvation, new creation, and so forth. But none of these are the center of the Bible because they lose their meaning without Christ. If there is no Christ, then there is really no kingdom to talk about (Matt. 25:34). If there is no Christ, then there is no creation (Jn. 1:3; Col. 1:16) nor new creation (2 Cor. 5:17). If there is no Christ, there is no salvation (Matt. 20:28). The diversity of the Bible is unified in Christ. He is the center that holds all of the biblical data together. While the covenants might be the relationship between God and his people, and the kingdom of God is certainly his pervasive rule over all people, yet the fullest expression of God and his glory comes not in a covenant but in a person, in the unique person and work of the Lord Jesus Christ. This is why covenants are important they teach us about Jesus.

Graeme Goldsworthy put it this way: "[Jesus] showed himself to be the real subject of biblical theology that had been developing ever since human beings first received revelation from God. He thus established biblical theology as the key to understanding Scripture, for he is the salvation historical event that gives significance to all others."[2] There is no use in going any further in our study of the Bible if we do not see how the Bible in its many parts connects to the person the Bible is about.

There is a church in Calcutta where a famous missionary once served. William Carey was the minister of Circular Road Baptist Chapel. Behind the pulpit is a worn-out chair where he and the ministers after him sat. From the chair the minister can see a sign, (maybe it's on the pulpit; I'm not exactly sure where the sign is). The sign is a quotation from John 12:21, "Sir, we would see Jesus." What a wonderful reminder for pastors. It is a reminder for all of us, really. When you study your Bible, when you are doing your "Through the Bible Reading in a Year" and you are in those long Levitical passages or the genealogies with those hard-to-pronounce names, remember that the Word of God is about the Living Word, the Word made flesh. Christ ought to be discovered in the Old Testament and there is more of Christ in our Old Testament Bible than the New Testament writers cite. Covenants are about Christ because both Old and New Testaments are about him.

---

[2] Graham Goldsworthy, *Preaching the Whole Bible As Christian Scripture* (Grand Rapids: Eerdmans, 2000), 52.

CHAPTER EIGHT

Hebrews' testimony

> ¹Long ago, at many times and in many ways, God spoke to our fathers by the prophets, ²but in these last days he has spoken to us by his Son, whom he appointed the heir of all things, through whom also he created the world. ³He is the radiance of the glory of God and the exact imprint of his nature, and he upholds the universe by the word of his power. After making purification for sins, he sat down at the right hand of the Majesty on high, ⁴having become as much superior to angels as the name he has inherited is more excellent than theirs." (Heb. 1:1-4)

We begin with this text for two reasons. In the first place, one cannot help but notice that the writer of Hebrews is interested in the covenants. The Greek word for covenant is *diathēkē*. If you want to see how the New Testament understands the covenants of the Old Testament, let me suggest you read the book of Hebrews. The word is found thirty times in the New Testament, fourteen of which are in Hebrews. Almost half of the occurrences of this word are in Hebrews. The writer is interested in showing, among other things, how the covenants are about Christ.

But it is more than just covenants speaking about Christ. Notice the time frame indicator in verse one: "God has spoken at various times." He did not communicate all at once; he communicated gradually. He spoke in "various ways." The Jews recognized this, and so they divided the corpus of Scripture into three sections: the Law, the Prophets, and the Writings. I take that to be part of the thrust here—God communicates in various ways. Imagine what the Bible would be like if God only communicated through wisdom literature like the book of Proverbs. God wrote in various times and used various styles to communicate his word, and he spoke in various ways: sometimes through visions and dreams; he spoke face to face with Moses on Mount Sinai; and through prophets, priests, and kings in Israel.

Then in verses 1 through 4 we have the sweep of redemptive history from the time of God's earliest revelation given to the forefathers and prophets to the time of Christ. Who is the Lord speaking of? He is speaking of His Son. What is God attesting to according to these verses? He is attesting to the supremacy and preeminence of His Son.

The remainder of chapter 1 consists primarily of citations from the Old Testament, *all* of which teach us about Christ. The author has carefully selected from the three sections of the Old Testament. In verse 5 there are citations from Psalm 2 and 1 Chronicles 17:13. In verse 6 we have references to Deuteronomy 32:43 and Psalm 97. In verse 9 and verse 11 we have citations and allusions to Isaiah. We have the Law, we have the Prophets, and we have the Writings being used by God to bring glory to his Son.

It is one thing to say that we can find interesting things about Jesus in the Law, the Prophets, and the Writings; it is quite another thing to say that all the Law, the Writings, and the Prophets are about Jesus. Is it the case that *all* of the Old Testament teaches us about God's work in the Lord Jesus Christ, or is it that *some* of the Old Testament is about God's work in Christ?

John's testimony

Let's answer that question with Jesus' own words found in John 5. In John 5, Jesus has healed a man on the Sabbath day, and his authority was challenged. To some, Jesus appeared to be setting aside the fourth commandment:

> ^{30} I can do nothing on my own. As I hear, I judge, and my judgment is just, because I seek not my own will but the will of him who sent me. ^{31} If I alone bear witness about myself, my testimony is not deemed true. ^{32} There is another who bears witness about me, and I know that the testimony that he bears about me is true. ^{33} You sent to John, and he has borne witness to the truth. ^{34} Not that the testimony that I receive is from man, but I say these things so that you may be saved. ^{35} He was a burning and shining lamp, and you were willing to rejoice for a while in his light. ^{36} But the testimony that I have is greater than that of John. For the works that the Father has given me to accomplish, the very works that I am doing, bear witness about me that the Father has sent me. ^{37} And the Father who sent me has himself borne witness about me. His voice you have never heard, his form you have never seen, ^{38} and you do not have his word abiding in you, for you do not believe the one whom he has sent. ^{39} You search the Scriptures because you think that in them you have eternal life; and it is they that bear witness about me, ^{40} yet you refuse to come to me that you may have life. ^{41} I do not receive glory from people. ^{42} But I know that you do not have the love of God within you. ^{43} I have come in my Father's name, and you do not receive me. If another comes in his own name, you will receive him. ^{44} How can you believe, when you receive glory from one another and do not seek the glory that comes from the only God? ^{45} Do not think that I will accuse you to the Father. There is one who accuses you: Moses, on whom you have set your hope. ^{46} For if you believed Moses, you would believe me; for he wrote of me. ^{47} But if you do not believe his writings, how will you believe my words?

In vv. 32-33 Jesus sums up the work of John the Baptist, "There is another who bears witness about me, and I know that the testimony he bears about me is true" (v. 32). Then in v. 37 Jesus describes a greater testimony than John's, "The Father who sent me has himself borne witness about me." They have not heard the father's voice nor seen his form (v. 37), but they did have his word, and it is precisely here that Jesus crystallizes their problem, "You search the Scriptures because you think that in them you have eternal life; *and it is they that bear witness about me*, yet you refuse to come to me that you may have life" (vv. 39-40, emphasis mine).

As an aside, I can't imagine anything much more jarring than these words. God gave Israel Scripture, and they were the arbiters of God's truth. Hadn't he given them prophets and priests to instruct the covenant people, and yet Jesus can look them in the face and say, "You search those Scriptures in vain." Why? Because Scripture bears witness about him. Did you notice that Jesus said, *Scriptures* not *Scripture*? Jesus is saying that all the Scriptures, not just the five books of Moses, but also the Writings and the Prophets bear witness about him.

Finally, vv. 45-47 give us one of the most compelling reasons to read and interpret the Bible with an eye to the person and work of Jesus Christ:

> [45] Do not think that I will accuse you to the Father. There is one who accuses you: Moses, on whom you have set your hope. [46] For if you believed Moses, you would believe me; *for he wrote of me.* [47] But if you do not believe his writings, how will you believe my words?" (emphasis mine)

You won't understand the law of Moses without Christ. Moses writes about Jesus. He says Moses writes about me. Israel can't say, "No, Jesus you have it all wrong; Moses wrote about Abraham, Isaac, Jacob, and the nation of Israel, not you." By failing to believe Jesus, they align themselves against the law of Moses and find themselves accused and convicted for this crime. Even though the law was handed down to Israel, and Israel was to obey it; nevertheless, if they thought that their law keeping was the way to life, then they were deceived because the law was not given to point them in direction of greater effort. Moses gave them the law to point them to Christ.

Neither Jesus nor the writers of the New Testament are denying that the Old Testament speaks about the people and events of that era. The Old Testament has much to say about a good many things, but if we interpret it without an eye for Christ, we are missing the key figure of the Bible. If I can borrow from Michael Horton, he says that Abraham, Moses, Joshua, David, Samson, and the nation of Israel are not the headliners of the Bible. God is, especially as he works redemption for his people through Jesus Christ. Jesus is center stage in both testaments. Having underscored the Christ-centeredness of Old Testament Scripture, we now move on to the exodus.

The story of God's salvation

The book of Exodus begins by picking up the story of Abraham's offspring that had gone down to Egypt because of a seven-year famine and remained there for four hundred years. Abraham went from having one son of promise to many children of the promise. "But the children of Israel were fruitful and increased abundantly, multiplied and grew exceedingly mighty; and the land was filled with them" (Ex. 1:7).

Not only have the Israelites become numerous, they are mighty (Ex. 1:8). In an attempt for domination and control, the Egyptians mistreat Abraham's offspring (Ex. 1:8-14). The king of Egypt summons the midwives and commands them to kill the male Hebrew children (Ex. 1:5-22). The situation is desperate. A woman gives birth to a son, Moses, who is himself rescued from the threat of death (Ex. 2). When Moses is older, he kills an Egyptian. His attempt to cover the body is discovered, and Moses flees to Midian (Ex. 2). As much as he would prefer to stay in Midian, the Lord has other plans. After encountering God in the blaze of the burning bush, Moses packs up his things and returns to Egypt. He does not go unequipped because the leprous hand and the slithering staff are signs for all to see (Ex. 4:1-9). God also has other miraculous signs for Egypt. Moses doesn't just bring signs and wonders; he brings the word of the Lord. God has a message for the King of Egypt, "Thus says the LORD, Israel is my firstborn son, and I say to you, let my son go that he may serve me" (Ex. 4:22-23). One after the other, the miraculous signs come crashing down upon the land of Egypt reducing it to ruin (Ex. 4-12). The miraculous signs, ten of them in all, end with the death of the firstborn (Ex. 12:29-30), and when the firstborn are put to death, God's son is released. But before the tenth sign is carried out, instructions for a celebration are given. This moment of redemption is commemorated by the feast of Passover (Ex. 12). The Passover lambs are slain, and their blood is smeared across the lintel and the doorposts of their homes (Ex. 12:22).

After they leave Egypt, they travel through the wilderness (Ex. 13:18) only to be confronted with a problem. The Red Sea lay in front of them as a barrier while the army of Pharaoh closes in behind them (Ex. 14). They are trapped, and their only options are to return to slavery or to start swimming. God's plan is always better. As the strong east wind blows all night, the Lord makes a way for his people through the sea. He parts that

CHAPTER EIGHT

great body of water, and his people walk on dry land. Israel is "baptized into Moses in the cloud and in the sea" (1 Cor. 10:2). The apostle Paul describes Israel walking through the sea as a baptism. Israel crosses safely, Pharaoh is not so fortunate. Blinded by his foolish heart, he enters in after them and is overtaken by the waters of God's judgment.

Israel, the son of God are free. They are free to go and meet their father and worship him. Journeying on their way to that first corporate worship service, the Lord gives them provisions. He rains bread from heaven (Ex. 16). Sustained by God's generous provisions, Israel arrives at Mount Sinai (Ex. 19).

This is the moment they had been waiting for. The sight of the Lord descending upon the mountain in the cloud and the sound of his voice thundering strike fear in his people (Ex. 20:18). Their mediator, Moses, goes up onto the mountain and received the law. Upon hearing that law and swearing to do all that God commanded, Israel enters into a covenant with God (Ex. 20ff). As Moses sprinkles the people with blood, he says, "Behold the blood of the covenant" (Ex. 24:8). Again Moses climbs the mountain and remains there forty days. As the days wear on, the enthusiasm wears thin, and God's covenant people grow impatient. When Moses receives the instructions for the place of worship at the top of the mountain, a golden calf is being worshipped at the foot of the mountain (Ex. 32). It is only because of the grace of God, bound up in his covenant promises made to Abraham, Isaac, and Jacob, that Moses could plead and Israel be spared (Ex. 32:13). Though broken, the covenant is renewed (Ex. 34). An encounter with such a holy God as the Lord leaves an impression upon a person ushered into his presence. In Moses' case, it is a physical impression and when he comes down the mountain, his face shines white (Ex. 34:29-35).

Moving to the book of Numbers, the spies are sent into Canaan, twelve of them to be exact (Num. 13:2). Yet Israel's rebellion runs deep. God's sons refuse to enter and take possession of the land God had given them (Num. 14). With the exception of Joshua and Caleb, the first generation is consigned to wander in the wilderness and die there (Num. 14:26-38). Though Israel is not deterred and continues to rebel against the Lord (Num. 14:39ff.), God's decree stands, "According to the number of the days in which you spied out the land, forty days, a year for each day, you shall bear your iniquity forty years, and you shall know my displeasure" (Num. 14:34).

For forty years, Israel learns God's displeasure, bearing their iniquity until the first generation is placed in the ground. Even Moses, the mediator between God and his people must die. In the Lord's kindness another leader is appointed, and Joshua is commissioned to lead God's people into the Promised Land (Josh. 1). Once again, spies are sent to look at that land, but this time it is only two men (Josh. 2:1), and they return with a good report just like Joshua and Caleb did under Moses. Under Joshua's command, God parts the Jordan River, and Israel crosses into his inheritance (Josh. 3). The covenant of circumcision is re-instituted (Josh. 5) before Israel begins conquering the nations, "All the good things God had promised them were brought to pass, not one word of them failed" (Josh. 23:14).

The commitment that God made to Abraham, Isaac, and Jacob, the covenant bond that he had established with the patriarchs, was not set aside. Abraham had offspring and his offspring possessed the Promised Land (Gen. 15:16). God's word did not fail but accomplished all that he purposed on one level, yet there was a deeper level and meaning. When God's light shone upon Israel, a shadow of the good things to come was cast.

Matthew's gospel of Exodus

The New Testament begins with the words "The book of the genealogy of Jesus Christ, the Son of David, the Son of Abraham" (Matt. 1:1). Matthew begins with three names: Jesus, David, and Abraham. Matthew traces their lineage beginning with Abraham and ending with Jesus. Following the main figures of the genealogy, it reads Jesus, David, Abraham, Abraham, David, Jesus (Matt. 1:2, 6, 16). Standing in the center is Abraham. Matthew is going to show us how the covenant with Abraham can only be fulfilled in Christ. There is an emphasis upon Abraham because of the covenant made with him (Gen. 15). The blessings that flow from the Abrahamic covenant are because Christ is the center of that covenant, not Abraham. Now we observe how Abraham's history and his descendants' history are not the goal; the goal is Christ. God gives Abraham's elderly wife a son when she is well past the age of childbearing, and the Lord gives Mary a Son even though she is a virgin.

In chapter two Jesus is taken from the land of Israel down into Egypt. Why? Because he is in danger. Once again the Jewish males are threatened with death by another king. Matthew tells us that like Israel, Jesus' departure was also under the cover of night (Matt. 2:14). Jesus' parents sought refuge not from Egypt but in Egypt, which raises the question, who is the real Egypt in this story?

Without any explanation Matthew goes from the infancy of Jesus to his adulthood. A messenger is sent with an ultimatum, "Repent, or be judged" (Matt. 3:2, 7-10). Jesus goes to the Jordan River and is baptized in the waters (Matt. 3:13-17). As Israel of old, Jesus goes through the

CHAPTER EIGHT

waters as the voice of heaven declares, "This is my beloved son, with whom I am well pleased" (Matt. 3:17). Could it be that the pleasure for this son is a result of the son's obedience rather than a cry for mercy because of the awareness of sins? The reader does not have to wait long to obtain the answer.

Once Jesus goes through the water, he enters the wilderness (Matt. 4:1ff.). He goes into the wilderness to be tested. The reader is once again reminded of Israel's forty years in the wilderness. Jesus has this in mind too as he counters Satan's advance with citations from Deuteronomy, and he proves himself a faithful son. What does Jesus do after he emerges victoriously from the wilderness? We find him climbing up a mountain, and from that mountain he delivers a new law or, as it is often called, The Sermon on the Mount (Matt. 5-7).

In chapters 8 and 9, Matthew records a number of miracles. I would bet you could guess how many are found there. As Moses performed ten miraculous signs, so also Matthew focuses our attention upon the signs performed by Christ—ten miracles, ten signs. Here we see God reversing the mighty judgments that took place in the land of Egypt. Ten miracles! Jesus is the greater Moses; he gives the greater law and performs the gracious and greater signs!

In chapter 10, Matthew goes from signs to sending. Jesus sent out his disciples, twelve, to be exact. How many were sent out to spy the Promised Land in the time of Moses? Twelve. In Matthew 12:38 and chapter 16:1 the Jews demand a sign. To paraphrase, "Give us a sign that we might know that we can follow you." Embedded between those two requests, we find Jesus feeding the multitudes. Five thousand are fed in chapter 14 and the four thousand in chapter 15. Here is the manna, the bread of heaven. In chapter 17, Jesus went up onto a mountain and was transfigured. His face was glowing like the sun, and his clothes were radiant white. Who appears with Him on the mountain but Elijah and Moses? When the cloud appears and the voice from the cloud thunders over them, the disciples were afraid (Matt. 17:6) as was Israel when they experienced the cloud and voice.

In chapters 21-25 Jesus entered into the epicenter of the Promised Land. He went into Jerusalem, into the temple, but the leaders rejected him. The oracle of judgment, the covenant curse, was pronounced against the temple, "Not one stone will be left upon another" (Matt. 24:2). In chapter 26, Jesus is celebrating something with his disciples; what is he celebrating? None other than the Passover. Passover tells the story of Israel's dramatic deliverance from Egypt. Jesus celebrated the Passover and instituted the Lord's Supper. As Jesus instituted this new feast for his people, the language of the covenant is invoked, "This is the blood of the covenant" (Matt. 26:28). "This is my body... this is my blood..." This is how the covenant is going to be fulfilled. Blood is going to be shed, but this time it will not stain the doorposts of houses but the wood of the cross.

As Moses offers himself as a substitute on the top of the mountain (Ex. 32:32), Jesus offers himself at the top of Golgotha as a sacrifice (Matt. 26:33). And Christ's sacrifice is accepted (Matt. 27:45,51-53). Matthew's gospel ends with the Great Commission (Matt. 28:19). Now the Israel of God will go out, and instead of conquering the nations with a sword, they are given the gospel: "Go out and make disciples of all nations." As Matthew opened with a reminder of the covenant promises made to Abraham, so his gospel closes with the picture of the offspring of Abraham. They are commissioned by the promised offspring of Abraham to go out into the nations with the gospel and see God fulfill his covenant promises to Abraham, that his descendants would be as many as the stars in heaven.

As it was in the beginning

The story of redemption has always been in Christ. From beginning to end, the story of the Bible is Jesus' story. The covenants, the promises, the law, the prophets, faithfulness, sacrifices, land—all declares beforehand what God will do in sending his Son into the world. No wonder Jesus said, "For if you believed Moses, you would believe me; for he wrote about me" (Jn. 5:46). Israel's story was the outworking of God's covenants with the patriarchs and with Adam before them. This covenant story was anticipating the salvation of the new covenant that Jesus brought with his blood-bought sacrifice. Israel's Scripture anticipates Jesus' words; Israel's sacrificial system and Israel's expulsion from the Promised Land anticipated Jesus' being cut off from the land of living. Israel's life in the Promised Land anticipated the life of the Son of God who opens the way to his redeemed people to enter into the new heavens and new earth through the blood of the covenant, prepared before the foundation of the world, declared in the types and shadows of the Old Testament, and illuminated and revealed in the New Testament. The history shaped by the covenant is truly his covenant story.

The Exodus	
Old	New
Nations blessed through Abraham's son (Gen. 12; 13; 15)	Book of generations, Jesus, David, Abraham (Matt. 1:1)
Abraham's offspring fruitful and	Abraham's descendants (Matt.

multiplying (Ex. 1:7)	1:2-17)
King of Egypt wants to kill Israelite males (Ex. 1:8-14)	King Herod kills male children in Bethlehem (Matt. 2:16-18)
Moses is born and rescued (Ex.2)	Jesus' birth (Matt. 1:18-25)
Moses kills an Egyptian and escapes to Midian (Ex. 2)	Jesus escapes to Egypt (Matt. 2:13-14)
God meets Moses at Mt. Horeb (Ex. 3)	
Moses performs ten signs and wonders (Ex. 4-12)	Jesus performs ten signs and wonders (Matt. 8-9)
Israel celebrates Passover (Ex. 12)	Jesus celebrates Passover with disciples (Matt. 26)
Death of firstborn; Israel released (Ex. 12:29ff.)	Jesus dies; Israel released (Matt. 27:50; 52-53)
Through Red Sea (Ex. 14; baptized into Moses (1 Cor 10:2))	Jesus goes through the waters (Matt. 3:13-17)
God rains down bread from heaven/manna (Ex. 16)	Jesus feeds 5,000 (Matt. 14:13-20, 4,000 (Matt. 15:29ff.)
Israel at Mt. Sinai (Ex. 19)	
Moses on the mountain receives the law (Ex. 20ff.)	Jesus gives the law on the mountain (Matt. 5-7)
Blood of the covenant sprinkled on the people (Ex. 24:8)	This is *my* blood of the covenant (Matt.26:28)
Golden calf is worshipped below (Ex. 32)	
The covenant renewed (Ex. 34)	
Moses' face shining (Ex. 34:35)	Jesus is transfigured on mountain (Matt. 17:1-8)
Twelve spies go into the Promised Land, 2 by 2 (Num. 13)	Jesus sends out twelve apostles, two by two (Matt. 10)
Israel refuses to believe and enter the land (Num. 14:1-11)	Jesus is rejected by leaders (Matt. 21-25)
The generation will perish (Num. 14:26ff.)	This generation will perish (Matt. 23:36)
The generation will perish (Num. 14:26ff.)	This generation will perish (Matt. 23:36; 24:34)
Forty days plus forty years in wilderness (Num. 14:34)	Jesus in the wilderness forty days (Matt. 4:1-11)

Moses dies, Joshua is commissioned (Josh. 1)	Jesus dies and is raised (Matt. 27:50; 28:1-10)
2 spies sent out (Josh. 2)	
God parts the Jordan River (Josh. 3)	Jesus baptized in the Jordan River (Matt. 3:13-17)
Covenant circumcision and Passover observed (Josh. 5)	Jesus celebrates Passover with disciples (Matt. 26)
Israel begins to conquer nations (Josh. 6-11)	Disciples go out; nations conquered by gospel (Matt. 28:19)

Study Questions:

1. How can Jesus be the center of the Bible?
2. What are the benefits of reading the Old Testament in a Christ-centered way?
3. Are there disadvantages to reading the Old Testament without a Christ-centered focus?
4. Why did Jesus retrace the steps of Old Testament Israel?

Chapter 9: Covenant Initiation: Baptism

> So does the blood of Christ by the power of the Holy Spirit internally sprinkle the soul, cleanse it from its sins, and regenerate us from children of wrath unto children of God. Not that this is effected by the external water, but by the sprinkling of the precious blood of the Son of God; who is our Red Sea, through which we must pass to escape the tyranny of Pharaoh, that is, the devil, and to enter into the spiritual land of Canaan. (Belgic Confession, Art. 34)

Just as circumcision was a knife drawn in judgment yet "passed over" the recipient by cutting away merely the foreskin, in baptism too, we come under the sword of divine judgment. In this event, however, we are entirely dedicated to judgment in order to be entirely raised in newness of life (Rom. 6:1-11).What is signified and sealed in baptism is nothing less than the eschatological judgment of the last day: our curse in Adam swallowed by our blessing in Christ.[1]

The valley of decision

As the sun rises, the silhouette of a man can be seen down by the river. His garment is rough camel's hair, and a leather belt is his only accessory. His diet is locust and wild honey (Mk. 1:6). His leathery face bears resemblance to those who make their home in the wilderness. His voice cries out as people come down the mountainside to get a look at this strange spectacle. The wilderness is a strange place to attract a listening audience when the cities are bustling with people, but folks are drawn all the same. It had long been understood that the wilderness would be a place of special importance, the entryway for God himself (Isa. 40:3).

The rough garment, leather belt, and the wilderness tell the nation that this is no desert nomad (2 Ki. 1:8). This is the prophet spoken of by Isaiah. This is the voice calling out in the wilderness to prepare the

---

[1] Michael Horton, *The Christian Faith: A Systematic Theology for Pilgrims on the Way* (Grand Rapids: Zondervan; 2011), 789-790.

people for the coming of Yahweh. As the people come, they are confronted with the announcement that the kingdom of heaven is about to arrive. Words that warm the heart also send a chill down the spine. "Repent, for the kingdom of heaven is at hand." The kingdoms of the world had not ruled according to heaven's principles. Repentance is needed if mercy is to be sought. The breach of the covenant left Israel like Jericho, without walls, exposed before the coming of the Lord with his heavenly hosts.

However not everyone is convinced this was the case. Humility and repentance are not the response of the leaders of Israel who claim Abraham as their father (Matt. 3:9). To be found without the fruits of repentance is to find oneself without escape, and so John warns them (Matt. 3:8). The axe has already been laid at the root of the tree (Matt. 3:10). The root is now exposed; the dirt around it removed, and the axe is already laid next to its target. Every tree not bearing the fruit of repentance would experience the axe blade and the flame. The nation stands on the brink of the abyss.

To the images of axe and fire, water is added. People approach John and experience the water poured out upon their bodies. It is a sign that only the repentant will pass through the eschatological waters without harm. For the eyes of faith the waters are a sign of God's mercy. For those with no spiritual insight, the waters signal their undoing. As noted by Meredith Kline:

> The most memorable divine judgments of all covenant history had been trials by water ordeal and since John was sent to deliver the ultimatum of divine judgment, it does not appear too bold an interpretation of the baptismal sign of his mission to see in it a symbolic water ordeal, a dramatic enactment of the imminent messianic judgment. In such a visualization of the coming judgment John will have been resuming the prophetic tradition of picturing the messianic mission as a second Red Sea judgment (and so a water ordeal).[2]

There could be no question that John's baptism was a symbol-laden portrayal of the coming baptism to be performed by the covenant Lord. Fire is once again prophetically inserted into Israel's future; "He will baptize you with the Holy Spirit and fire" (Matt. 3:11). His mission is simple; evil must be purged from his kingdom. The repentant wheat would be spared; the tares await their day in eternal fire (Matt. 3:12), and

---

[2] M. G. Kline, *By Oath Consigned* (Grand Rapids: Eerdmans; 1968), 56.

there is no third choice. The one who comes is mightier than John. He comes to destroy with Spirit and fire.

As Jesus steps into the water, John's head begins to spin. How could Jesus step into these waters and submit himself to this baptism, bowing his head under the flood of God's judgment when he is the one who is supposed to unleash the fire of the Holy Spirit upon his enemies? But Jesus said to him, "Let it be so now, for thus it is fitting for us to fulfill all righteousness." It was then that he consented (Matt. 3:15). Before this sign of the covenant could ever be a means of grace for Israel, it must first be a sign and seal of the covenant curse for Jesus. The baptism of John identified the king of the kingdom who was bringing eschatological (heavenly) judgment. Little did John know that the king would first have to undergo this judgment himself on behalf of his covenant-breaking people. No wonder he stumbled at the thought:[3]

> Jesus' reception of John's baptism can be more easily understood on this approach. As covenant Servant, Jesus submitted in symbol to the judgment of the God of the covenant in the waters of baptism. But for Jesus, as the Lamb of God, to submit to the symbol of judgment was to offer himself up to the curse of the covenant. By his baptism, Jesus was consecrating himself unto his sacrificial death in the judicial ordeal of the cross.[4]

It will take nothing less than Christ undergoing the judgment of death, symbolized by the waters of baptism, to accomplish the verdict that is rendered for our justification (Rom. 4:25) and resurrection from the dead (1 Pet. 3:21).[5] Water can be both life-sustaining and life-ending as the Bible repeatedly affirms (Deut. 11:11; Neh. 9:15; Isa. 44:3; Gen. 7:11-24; Pss. 46:3; 69:2; 93:3). The context and content of John's preaching assures us that it is this latter meaning that Jesus had come to experience.

---

[3] The startled response (Matt. 3:14) followed by his bewildered request for clarification (Matt. 11:2-3) suggests that John expected the arrival of the king in judgment, or as the prophets before him had declared, the great and dreadful day of the Lord (Isa. 13:6, 9; Jer. 46:10; Joel 1:15; 2:11; Amos 5:18-21; Obad. 1:15; Zeph. 1:14-18). Malachi prophesied that Elijah would be sent before that great and dreadful day (Mal. 4:5).

[4] Kline, By Oath Consigned, 58.

[5] Water can be both life-sustaining and life-threatening as the bible repeatedly affirms (Deut. 11:11; Neh. 9:15; Isa. 44:3; Gen. 7:11-24; Psa. 46:3; 69:2; 93:3).

As the covenant Lord pressed forward in his ministry, he did not deny that he had come to cast fire upon the earth, "I came to cast fire on the earth, and would that it were already kindled!" (Lk. 12:49). But Christ's covenant obedience required something dreadful of him; before the fires of judgment could be released upon the world, he must first undergo them for the sake of his covenant people–an event which he likened to baptism. "I have a baptism to be baptized with, and how great is my distress until it is accomplished!" (Lk. 12:50). Richard Gaffin writes, "To save his people the Christ must propitiate that justly deserved divine wrath, by identifying with them in their guilt and enduring judgment for them; the Messiah is a judicial sin-bearer."[6] Jesus comes to cast fire upon the earth but because of the covenant of grace, this fire can only be released upon his enemies after Jesus had extinguished the fires of hell upon the cross for his friends.

After darkness, light

Only after the baptism of judgment upon the cross could Jesus say to his disciples on the mountain top, "Go therefore and make disciples of all nations, baptizing them in the name of the Father and of the Son and of the Holy Spirit" (Matt. 28:19). God removed the curse of the covenant of works from his people and placed his triune name upon them in baptism.

In the rite of baptism, God sets his covenant sign upon his people setting them apart from the world. Baptism is God's official, public declaration that *by faith* the person baptized is married to another (Rev. 21:2, 9). Baptism is the entryway into the visible church (Acts 2:41). But it is more than an outward sign. The same apostle who speaks of the Lord's Supper as a real communing with the body and blood of Christ (1 Cor. 10:16-17) can also speak of baptism as burial and resurrection with Christ (Col. 2:12), putting *on* Christ (Gal. 3:27), engrafting *into* Christ (Rom. 6:5), by the washing and renewal of the Holy Spirit (Tit. 3:5). Baptism points to the blood of Christ which cleanses us from all our sins and, says Calvin, "the mortification of our flesh, which rests upon participation in his death and through which believers are reborn into newness of life and into the fellowship of Christ."[7]

---

[6] Richard Gaffin, "Justification in Luke-Acts," D.A. Carson, ed., *Right with God. Justification in the Bible and the World* (Paternoster/Baker, 1992), 111.

[7] John Calvin, *Institutes of the Christian Religion*, ed. John T. McNeill, trans. Ford Lewis Battles, Library of Christian Classics (London: SCM, 1960), 4.16.2.

Baptism is a sign of all these saving graces promised to believers. But as Calvin reminds us it is not an empty sign:

> Now the Apostles are wont to draw an argument from the Sacraments, to prove that which is there exhibited under a figure, because it ought to be held by believers as a settled principle, that God does not sport with us by unmeaning figures, but inwardly accomplishes by his power what he exhibits by the outward sign; and therefore, baptism is fitly and truly said to be "the washing of regeneration." The efficacy and use of the sacraments will be properly understood by him who shall connect the sign and the thing signified, in such a manner as not to make the sign unmeaning and inefficacious, and who nevertheless shall not, for the sake of adorning the sign, take away from the Holy Spirit what belongs to him. Although by baptism wicked men are neither washed nor renewed, yet it retains that power, so far as it relates to God, because, although they reject the grace of God, still it is offered to them. But here Paul addresses believers, in whom baptism is always efficacious, and in whom, therefore, it is properly connected with its truth and efficacy. But by this mode of expression we are reminded that, if we do not wish to annihilate holy baptism, we must prove its efficacy by "newness of life." (Romans 6:4.)[8]

Likewise the Westminster Divines declared that:

> The efficacy of Baptism is not tied to that moment of time wherein it is administered; yet not withstanding, by the right use of this ordinance, the grace promised is not only offered but really exhibited, *and conferred*, by the Holy Ghost, to such (whether of age or infants) as that grace belongeth unto, according to the counsel of God's own will, in His appointed time. (Westminster Confession of Faith 28:6, emphasis mine)

Who is doing the speaking?

Baptism is a sign and a seal of the covenant of grace with all of its blessings located in Christ and applied to us by the Holy Spirit. In baptism we are identified as belonging wholly to God and are set apart from the world. It is God's *visible word* to his covenant people. The meaning of baptism, as with every sacrament, is not our public declaration to follow Jesus. It is the Father's public declaration to make fallen sinners citizens of heaven by faith in Jesus Christ, through his

---

[8] John Calvin, *Commentary on Timothy, Titus, Philemon* (Grand Rapids: Baker, 2003), 333.

Spirit. Baptism is not a demonstration of our commitment to God; rather, baptism is a sign of God's commitment to fulfill his promises made to his Son in eternity (Eph. 1). This last point is the great divide. Once baptism becomes *my* public declaration of *my* decision to be a follower of Jesus, the meaning of baptism becomes clouded. Paul insists that baptism points to God's initiative, power and saving grace in Jesus:

> [3] Do you not know that all of us who have been baptized into Christ Jesus were baptized into his death? [4] We were buried therefore with him by baptism into death, in order that, just as Christ was raised from the dead by the glory of the Father, we too might walk in newness of life. [5] For if we have been united with him in a death like his, we shall certainly be united with him in a resurrection like his. (Rom 6:3-5)

> [11] In him also you were circumcised with a circumcision made without hands, by putting off the body of the flesh, by the circumcision of Christ, [12] having been buried with him in baptism, in which you were also raised with him through faith in the powerful working of God, who raised him from the dead. [13] And you, who were dead in your trespasses and the uncircumcision of your flesh, God made alive together with him, having forgiven us all our trespasses. (Col. 2:11-13)

Baptism is a sign and a seal of God's saving power to raise spiritually dead sinners to life by the powerful working of the Holy Spirit, who imparts faith to lay hold of Christ and cherish him forever. Baptism shows that salvation is entirely God-centered. It extols the God who brings salvation to those who never dreamt of seeking it. In baptism we are passive. We do not baptize ourselves. Baptism is a sign of Romans 9:16, "So then it depends not on human will or exertion but on God, who has mercy." Baptism is not an opportunity for celebrating the free choice of a sinner to accept Jesus as their Savior. No, it is an opportunity for the church to celebrate the choice of the triune God to rescue redeemed sinners by his Son and through his Spirit.

God drove this point home to me when I was a student at Westminster Seminary in California. Dr. Dennis Johnson was speaking to us about a baptism he had performed. He told us how he had held a little baby in his arms and then baptized that infant in the name of the Father, Son, and Holy Spirit. What an example, he told us, of total inability and sovereign grace. That baby couldn't ask to be baptized, couldn't get itself to church to receive it. The child was entirely passive as the water was poured upon its head; so also are the spiritual realities to which baptism points us. The meaning of baptism is to be discovered in God's saving work. Baptism is a visible proclamation of sovereign grace. It is a visible sign and seal of

God's power to bring dead sinners to life through the power of the gospel. God sovereignly calls, regenerates, and makes us willing and able to receive Christ as he is freely offered to us in the gospel (Westminster Shorter Catechism Q/A 31). As Herman Bavinck has put it:

> In baptism the Father witnesses to us that he makes an eternal covenant of grace with us and adopts us as his children and heirs (Gen. 17:7, 10; Acts 2:39). The Son assures us that he washes us in his blood and incorporates us into the fellowship of his death and resurrection (Rom. 6:3; Gal 3:27). The Holy Spirit assures us that he lives in us and sanctifies us to be members of Christ (1 Cor. 6:11; 12:13; Tit. 3:5).[9]

This last point opens up the important question: Who is to receive the sign of the covenant of grace and so be admitted as a member of the visible church? Is it for believers only, or are the children of believers also to receive the sign of baptism? The answer to this question will take us to the end of this chapter.

Infant baptism

In 1 Corinthians Paul reminded the factitious and fractured church of his single aim as he ministered among them:

> [10] I appeal to you, brothers, by the name of our Lord Jesus Christ, that all of you agree, and that there be no divisions among you, but that you be united in the same mind and the same judgment. [11] For it has been reported to me by Chloe's people that there is quarreling among you, my brothers. [12] What I mean is that each one of you says, "I follow Paul," or "I follow Apollos," or "I follow Cephas," or "I follow Christ." [13] Is Christ divided? Was Paul crucified for you? Or were you baptized in the name of Paul? [14] I thank God that I baptized none of you except Crispus and Gaius, [15] so that no one may say that you were baptized in my name. [16] (I did baptize also the household of Stephanas. Beyond that, I do not know whether I baptized anyone else.) [17] For Christ did not send me to baptize but to preach the gospel, and not with words of eloquent wisdom, lest the cross of Christ be emptied of its power. (1 Cor. 1:10-17)

I hope that it is abundantly clear in our exposition of the covenants and the signs and seals of those covenants (baptism and the Lord's

---

[9] Herman Bavinck, *Reformed Dogmatics*; 4 vols. (Grand Rapids: Baker; 2008), 4:519.

Supper), that the sacraments are powerless to save. Clearly, Paul did not see the sacraments as converting ordinances; otherwise, his ministry would have held a lot more water. The indispensable thing was not water, but word (v. 17). It would be unfair and unwise to assume that all who are convinced of infant baptism believe it to be a saving ordinance.

What we are convinced of is the organic unity of the Bible which reflects both continuity and discontinuity. Obviously there is discontinuity since you do not bring lambs to church to be sacrificed and so forth. But despite the changes that have occurred, there are some things that stay the same. *The gospel does not change.* As we read Scripture, we discover that every gospel doctrine has its roots in the Old Testament.

<u>Galatians 3:29</u> We are Abraham's offspring and heirs according to the promise (Isa. 51:2; 63:16).

<u>Philippians 3:3</u> We are the true circumcision (Gen. 17).

<u>Galatians 2:16</u> Justification is by faith not works (Gen. 15:6).

<u>Hebrews 9:15</u> The covenant mediator represents the people to God (Ex. 32:31-32).

We should at least be open to the possibility that the new covenant signs aren't introducing something new and foreign to the Old Testament.

Christ-centered covenants and signs

There is a certain biblical logic that we have tried to develop in our study of covenant theology. All covenants speak about Christ, and secondly, all covenant signs (sacraments) speak about Christ. The covenants we have looked at are the result of God's sovereign initiative. God makes covenants with his creatures, and he gives his people visible signs and seals of his covenant promises. In both covenant word and sign, God speaks about Christ.

In the Old Testament, God gave two covenant signs to his people. He gave circumcision, which could only be administered once (Gen. 17:9-14), and he gave his people the Passover meal, which was to be administered annually (Ex. 12:25-27). In the New Testament, God gives two signs: baptism, which by design is to be administered once (Matt. 28:19), and the Supper, which is to be administered frequently (Lk. 22:15-20).

As the New Testament makes clear, circumcision and Passover are no longer the covenant signs. The Lord's Supper replaces Passover (Lk. 22:19), and baptism replaces circumcision (Col. 2:11-12; Rom. 2:28-29). So far, I hope, so good.

What did circumcision signify? In Deuteronomy 30:6 Moses writes:

> [6] And the LORD your God will circumcise your heart and the heart of your offspring, so that you will love the LORD your God with all your heart and with all your soul, that you may live.

Circumcision was a sign of regeneration and faith (cf. Rom. 4:6-10). It was the covenant sign announcing that God would cut away what was dead and give life. What then does baptism signify? It signifies the washing and renewal of the Holy Spirit (Tit. 3:5) and spiritual life from the dead (Col. 2:12). This old covenant sign and its new covenant counterpart point to the same reality. Most notably, Paul brings both signs together and shows their unified meaning in Christ:

> [11] In him also you were circumcised with a circumcision made without hands, by putting off the body of the flesh, by the circumcision of Christ, [12] having been buried with him in baptism, in which you were also raised with him through faith in the powerful working of God, who raised him from the dead. [13] And you, who were dead in your trespasses and the uncircumcision of your flesh, God made alive together with him, having forgiven us all our trespasses (Col. 2:11-13)

Notice how Paul correlates the meaning:
Circumcision
"Putting off the body of flesh" = death (v. 11)
"By Christ" = alive (v. 13)

Baptism
"Buried with him" = death (v. 12)
"Raised with him" = life (v. 12)

Our first conclusion that can be drawn is that both circumcision and baptism point to the same realities of our death and resurrection in Christ. Baptism was not added because something different was being proclaimed in the new covenant; both signs signified and sealed the same truth.

Our true spiritual lineage

As members of Christ, we trace our spiritual heritage back to Abraham, not Sinai (Gal. 4:24-26). We are Abraham's offspring. We belong to the Abrahamic covenant because of Abraham's offspring, Christ Jesus:

> [29] And if you are Christ's, then you are Abraham's offspring, heirs according to promise. (Gal. 3:29)

As those who can claim Father Abraham as our own, we ask the question, what was the entryway into the Abrahamic covenant? The answer is circumcision. God gave Abraham circumcision as a sign of his covenant and a seal of his promises. Who then received the sign of the Abrahamic covenant, the covenant of grace?

> [9] And God said to Abraham, "As for you, you shall keep my covenant, you and your offspring after you throughout their generations. [10] This is my covenant, which you shall keep, between me and you and your offspring after you: Every male among you shall be circumcised. [11] You shall be circumcised in the flesh of your foreskins, and it shall be a sign of the covenant between me and you. [12] He who is eight days old among you shall be circumcised. Every male throughout your generations, whether born in your house or bought with your money from any foreigner who is not of your offspring, [13] both he who is born in your house and he who is bought with your money, shall surely be circumcised. So shall my covenant be in your flesh an everlasting covenant. (Gen. 17:9-13)

For centuries the covenant sign was given to believing adults and their male sons, most of whom received the sign of the covenant in infancy (Gen. 21:4; Acts 7:8). For those who insist upon a sharp separation between Jews and Gentiles, please take note that the sign of the covenant was not just for the Jews; it was for Gentiles as well. "Whether born in your house or bought with your money from any *foreigner who is not of your offspring*, both he who is born in your house and he who is bought with your money, shall surely be circumcised" (vv. 12-13; emphasis mine).

Interestingly, even *unbelievers* in Abraham's household were circumcised with the sign of the covenant:

> [18] And Abraham said to God, "Oh that Ishmael might live before you!" 19 God said, "No, but Sarah your wife shall bear you a son, and you shall call his name Isaac. I will establish my covenant with him as an everlasting covenant for his offspring after him... [23] Then Abraham took Ishmael his son and all those born in his house or bought with his money, every male among the men of Abraham's house, and he circumcised the flesh of their foreskins that very day, as God had said to him. (Gen. 17:18-19, 23)

Circumcision was a visible sign and seal that declared the promises of God, and it was given to Ishmael even though he would never claim those promises by faith. God refused to establish his covenant with Ishmael, and yet he was still a member of the visible community of faith.

Why is Ishmael given the sign of the covenant even though he will ultimately be excluded from the gracious realities signified by circumcision? Why does God command that all males born in Abraham's household receive the sign of the covenant? The answer is that God has always dealt with individuals and with their families. Think with me about the overarching narrative of the Bible. When Adam stood before God, he represented not only himself but the children to come after him. Noah goes into the ark, and his family goes with him. God blesses Abraham and includes his children in the sign of his covenant blessings. God spared Abraham's nephew Lot, and Lot's daughters are delivered with him. Jewish males are delivered out of the hand of the angel of death when the father puts blood over the doorposts. Joshua declares to Israel, "As for me *and my house*, we will serve the Lord" (Josh. 24:15). The history of redemption is the history of God's dealings with believing parents and their children.

This is the biblical principle that compels us to apply the covenant sign of baptism to our infants. Do we believe that it will save them? Of course not, only faith in the Lord Jesus Christ will save them. But we give them the sign because we stand in a line of *continuity* with the Old Testament saints and Father Abraham. As God charged his people to trust him and give the sign of his covenant to their infant sons, we do the same for our children.

God is sovereign, and he commanded that infant males be circumcised *before* they could demonstrate any evidence of saving faith. It is his sovereign initiative to save whomsoever he wills, but nowhere were the parents of children commanded to withhold the sign until they could be reasonably sure of God's election of their children. It will not do to say, "That was Israel, this is the church." Abraham is our spiritual father, and the promises made to him and his offspring are our promises that also belong to us and our offspring.

New Testament continuity

For thousands of years God had included children in the covenant of grace, and there is absolutely nothing in the New Testament that suggests that this practice of giving children of believers the sign and seal of God's covenant had ceased. In fact, we find that the New Testament carries on the theme of children being included in the covenant of God. When Peter preached his covenantal, Christ-centered sermon on the day of Pentecost, it was received with much enthusiasm:

> [37] Now when they heard this they were cut to the heart, and said to Peter and the rest of the apostles, "Brothers, what shall we do?" [38] And Peter said to them, "Repent and be baptized every one of you in the name of Jesus Christ for the forgiveness of your sins, and you will receive the gift of the Holy Spirit. [39] *For the promise is for you and for your children and for all who are far off,* everyone whom the Lord our God calls to himself." (Acts 2:37-39, emphasis mine)

The promise is "for you and your children." This is a uniquely Abrahamic way of putting it. That promise, Peter says, is for you *and your children*. Here we have direct evidence of continuity. It is the same promise, unfolding throughout the Old Testament, made to the same people (believers and their children), and applied to them in the covenant sign.

O. Palmer Robertson has an excellent way of showing the tension that would exist if the sign of the covenant was no longer available for the children of believers. He asks the question:

> How would the people hearing Peter's sermon on the Day of Pentecost have understood this statement about their children? The question may be answered partially by considering the kind of nursery facilities that were available. There were no nursery facilities. Children were considered a vital part of the worshiping community. For 2,000 years children had been in the covenant, having received the sign of the covenant. *Are the children to be put out of the covenant now? Having begun the Day of Pentecost with their children included in God's covenant promises, are they who believed Peter's sermon to end the day with their children outside the promises of the covenant?* Peter's assurance (is) that the promise (is) "for you and your children."[10]

It is precisely here that we wish to humbly ask our Baptist brothers and sisters to be consistent in applying their principles of interpretation (hermeneutics). Baptists have often asked paedobaptists (infant baptists) to produce a text that *commands* infants to be baptized. They say this knowing that there is no such text. We won't argue with the principle of interpretation; we will only ask that they be consistent. Before we talk about a command to baptize infants, our Baptist friends must first produce a text that *commands* children be removed from the covenant. Since children had been included in the covenant for thousands of years,

---

[10] O. Palmer Robertson, *Covenants: God's Way With His People* (Suwanee: Great Commission Publications; 2003), 62. Emphasis mine.

we would need to have a verse telling us that they must be removed from the covenant before we can withhold the sign of the covenant from them.

The issue is should the children now be *put out* of the covenant? That is different than saying children are to be *kept out* of the covenant. To be kept out of the covenant would mean that they had never been a part in the first place. From the very beginning God has *always* included children with their believing parents. Because we are Abraham's offspring (Gal. 3:29), we would need a command that says our children are now to be put outside the covenant. Think of the first gospel promise that Adam and Eve heard. What did God say to the serpent? He said, "I will put enmity between you and the woman." That is good news, but he did not stop there. "I will put enmity between your offspring and her offspring" (Gen. 3:15). This is a gospel promise of Christ, and it is a promise not only for Eve, but for her children too. And we would hasten to add that just like Eve, they also must lay hold of it by faith!

If something had changed after thousands of years of Old Testament history, it would be a matter of putting the children out who were once included, and we would need an explicit command to do so, and we don't have one. After nearly a thousand years with millions upon millions of children included in the covenant, don't you think it would be strange for Peter's listeners to hear him say, "The promise is for you *and your children*" but conclude that the sign of that promise is, *"Not for your children?"* How would that be a better covenant?

In summary form, the pertinent points are as follows:

1.) *In the Old Testament, did God include children in his covenant promises?* Yes.

2.) *Did God ever refuse children into Old Testament covenant membership?* No, even apostates like Ishmael and Esau were included.

3.) *Is the church separate from Israel, the old covenant people of God?* No (cf. Gen. 12:3; Gen. 17:4-6; Rom. 11:16-17; Eph. 2:15).

4.) *With the coming of Christ, did the apostle declare that children are to be put out of the covenant?* No (Acts 2:38-39).

We have good biblical-theological grounds to insist that the sign of the covenant should not be removed from our covenant children.[11]

---

[11] Should infants, too, be baptized? Yes. Infants as well as adults are in God's covenant and are his people. They, no less than adults, are promised the forgiveness of sin through Christ's blood and the Holy

Baptized households

We find additional confirmation of these biblical principles in the household baptisms recorded in the New Testament. There are ten New Testament accounts of baptisms recorded in the books of Acts and 1 Corinthians. Six of the ten baptisms refer to *households*.[12] We shouldn't just assume that we can understand the meaning of *house/household* independent of the Old Testament. As ample Old Testament passages show, the household consists of children and parents.[13]

The logic of the kingdom of God

When we look at Christ's teaching on the subject of the kingdom of God, it is clear that the kingdom of God is the sphere of the redeemed. Put succinctly, the kingdom of God is God's people, in God's place, under God's rule:[14]

> Blessed are you who are poor, for yours is the kingdom of God. (Lk. 6:20)

> I tell you, among those born of women none is greater than John. Yet the one who is least in the kingdom of God is greater than he. (Lk. 7:28)

> [27] But I tell you truly, there are some standing here who will not taste death until they see the kingdom of God." [28] Now

---

Spirit who produces faith. Therefore, by baptism, the mark of the covenant, infants should be received into the Christian church and should be distinguished from the children of unbelievers. This was done in the Old Testament by circumcision, which was replaced in the New Testament by baptism. (Heidelberg Catechism Lord's Day 27, Q/A 74).

Unto whom is baptism to be administered? Baptism is not to be administered to any that are out of the visible church, and so strangers from the covenant of promise, till they profess their faith in Christ, and obedience to him, but infants descended from parents, either both or but one of them professing faith in Christ, and obedience to him, are, in that respect, within the covenant, and to be baptized. (Westminster Larger Catechism 166)

[12] Robertson, *Covenants*, 67.
[13] Gen. 4:30; Gen. 7:1; 12:17; 18:19; 36:6; 45:8; 50:7-8; 45:11; Lev. 16:6, 11, 17; Deut. 6:22; 14:26; 15:20; 26:11; Josh. 4:15; Jud. 18:25; 1 Sam. 1:21; 25:6; 2 Sam. 9:9; 15:16; 19:42; 21:1, 4; 1 Ki. 16:7; 2 Ki. 8:1; Jer. 38:17.
[14] Graham Goldsworthy, *Preaching the Whole Bible as Christian Scripture* (Grand Rapids: Eerdmans; 2000), 87.

> about eight days after these sayings he took with him Peter and John and James and went up on the mountain to pray. ²⁹ And as he was praying, the appearance of his face was altered, and his clothing became dazzling white. (Lk. 9:27-29)
>
> But if it is by the finger of God that I cast out demons, then the kingdom of God has come upon you. (Lk. 11:20)
>
> And when Jesus saw that he answered wisely, he said to him, "You are not far from the kingdom of God." And after that no one dared to ask him any more questions. (Mk. 12:34)
>
> ²⁴ Jesus, seeing that he had become sad, said, "How difficult it is for those who have wealth to enter the kingdom of God! ²⁵ For it is easier for a camel to go through the eye of a needle than for a rich person to enter the kingdom of God." (Lk. 18:24-25)

As this short list on Jesus' teaching of the kingdom of God makes clear, the kingdom of God is nothing less than God's promised salvation. Entrance into the kingdom of God is the goal of the covenant and the hope of God's covenant people. What Jesus says about the relationship of the kingdom of God to children is important. As parents were bringing their little children and infants to Jesus, the disciples stopped them. The master is too busy. He is too busy preaching and teaching those who can understand. Jesus was anything but pleased. The disciples did not have his interests in mind:

> ¹⁶ But Jesus called them to him, saying, "Let the children come to me, and do not hinder them, for to such belongs the kingdom of God. ¹⁷ Truly, I say to you, whoever does not receive the kingdom of God like a child shall not enter it." (Lk. 18:16-17)

Pay careful attention to these words, "for to such belongs the kingdom of God." In the Bible we see the kingdom of God advancing through the covenants. It is basically the place of salvation. Jesus said that the kingdom of God *belongs to the children*. This place of blessing, joy, salvation, and fellowship with God *belongs to the children*. Why then would you exclude them from the sign of these blessings? Since the kingdom belongs to the children of believing parents, we submit that the covenant sign is for the children since the sign which identifies those who belong to the kingdom is for the children.

In Christ's kingdom there is a diversity of people and ages. The children belong to the visible church because they have always belonged to the people of God. Without a command to put them outside the covenant, we must insist that they will remain inside. Because the kingdom of God belongs to them, we apply the sign of baptism to their little heads. It is a precious reminder that Jesus loves his little elect children every bit as much as his elect people of older years.

Study Questions:

1. Why was Jesus baptized by John?
2. What did John's baptism symbolize?
3. What is Christian baptism a sign and seal of?
4. How does the Reformed view of baptism differ from other views of baptism?
5. Who is doing the declaring in baptism?
6. How does the covenant inform the recipients of baptism?
7. Why is the Abrahamic covenant important to the Reformed practice of infant baptism?
8. Why weren't the covenant children put out of the covenant at Pentecost?
9. How does baptism teach us about Jesus?

Chapter 10: Covenant Meal: The Lord's Supper

Who and why?

The year was 1992. It was a year where a new president of the United States was to be elected. This election was unusual because there was a third party who had more votes than the incumbent president and the Democratic nominee. President George Bush Senior and Bill Clinton had to face off with Ross Perot, and it was clear that Perot had the people behind him. The vice-presidential debate was a different matter. On stage next to Vice President Dan Quayle and Al Gore stood Admiral James Stockdale, Ross Perot's 1992 running mate. He was convinced that the vast majority of the American people had no idea who he was. He only found out a week before the debate that he would be taking part in it. His opening comments will go down in history: "Who am I, and why am I here?" The place roared. He said other things that evening, but no one remembers them.

"Who am I, and why am I here?" This might be a helpful way to start our approach to the subject of the sacrament of the Lord's Supper as a covenant meal and as a means of grace. My hunch is that Admiral Stockdale's observation might ring true for some. When the table of the Lord is set before you it is helpful to ask these two questions. Who am I? I am God's covenant child. Why am I here? Because God has appointed bread and wine so that I can be spiritually fed by the body and blood of Christ.[1] God is concerned that your body as well as your soul has food to

---

[1] How does the Lord's supper remind you and assure you that you share in Christ's one sacrifice on the cross and in all his gifts? In this way: Christ has commanded me and all believers to eat this broken bread and to drink this cup. With this command he gave this promise: First, as surely as I see with my eyes the bread of the Lord broken for me and the cup given to me, so surely his body was offered and broken for me and his blood poured out for me on the cross. Second, as surely as I receive from the hand of him who serves, and taste with my mouth the bread and cup of the Lord, given me as sure signs of Christ's body and blood, so surely he nourishes and refreshes my soul for eternal life with his crucified body and poured-out blood. (Heidelberg Catechism Lord's Day 28, Q/A 75)

eat. Jesus gave his body and blood. By faith we feed upon him in the Lord's Supper, and he, in turn, feeds our hungry and thirsty souls. If you consume bread and wine, they are yours, and once inside, your body absorbs it. Scripture teaches that we eat and drink Christ's body and blood by faith. His broken body and shed blood upon the cross are an atonement *for us* because *we* belong to him. My life is in him, and he is in me (Jn. 14:20; 17:23). That is where you are, and that is why there is a seat for you at the Lord's Table. We need more of Christ every day. As parents we do not give our children all the food they need for their adolescent lives in one sitting. So also the Lord Jesus invites us week after week to sit at his table and feast upon his goodness. He feeds us his body and his blood and gives to us his grace so that we might have strength to walk after him in newness of life.

Covenant eating and drinking

The command of the new covenant to eat Christ's flesh and drink his blood comes from John 6. That might seem like a strange place to talk about the sacrament of the Lord's Supper because clearly the feeding of the 5,000 took place *before* Jesus instituted the Lord's Supper. It has been repeatedly asked if John 6 is about the Lord's Supper. How could those hearing him understand what he was saying since the Lord's Supper had not yet been given? In fact, John's Gospel does not even give us the celebration of the Lord's Supper in the upper room.

Though many Bible-believing commentators reject a sacramental reference in John 6, it is a curious thing that so many of the Protestant confessions and catechisms seek to explain the meaning of the Lord's Supper by citing John 6.[2] The voices of the past cause us to stop and ponder why the sixth chapter of John was such an important text.

So then is John 6 sacramental in any sense? Calvin says that this chapter is not strictly speaking about the Lord's Supper, but he does qualify this remark by writing, "I acknowledge that there is nothing said here that is not figuratively represented, and actually bestowed on believers, in the Lord's Supper; and Christ even intended that the holy Supper should be, as it were, a seal and confirmation of this sermon."[3] About one hundred years ago F. D. Maurice said, "If you ask me then

---

[2] Heidelberg Catechism (Q/A 76,79), Belgic Confession (Art. 35), Westminster Larger Catechism (Q/A 174), the French Confession of Faith (Art. 36), The Scotch Confession (Art. 21) and the Second Helvetic Confession (Ch. 21).

[3] Keith Mathison, *Given For You* (Phillipsburg NJ: Presbyterian and Reformed, 2002), 221.

whether he is speaking of the Eucharist here, I should say 'no.' If you ask me where I can learn the meaning of the Eucharist, I should say 'nowhere so well as here.'"[4]

Points of contact with the Lord's Supper[5]

While John 6 is not strictly speaking about the Lord's Supper, I believe the meaning of Jesus' words coalesce with it. The setting is the feeding of the 5,000 in the wilderness, and John tells us that it is the time of Passover (Jn. 6:4). Only the Gospel of John gives us the words, "Behold the Lamb of God who takes away the sin of the world" (1:29, 36).

With Passover at hand (v. 4) the Passover Lamb arrives. The Israelites ate manna in the wilderness, and here the true bread of life drew near. John sets Jesus' discourse in the context of the Passover.

In verse 11, Christians present and past hear something that sounds very familiar. "Jesus then took the loaves, and when he had given thanks, he distributed them to those who were seated."[6] This miracle wasn't lost on the crowds as their intent to make him king shows. But this king will be exalted in a very different way. The next day the crowds go looking for him:

> [22] On the next day the crowd that remained on the other side of the sea saw that there had been only one boat there, and that Jesus had not entered the boat with his disciples, but that his disciples had gone away alone. [23] Other boats from Tiberias came near the place where they had eaten the bread after the Lord had given thanks. (Jn. 6:22-23)

Why doesn't John say this was the place where Jesus performed the miracle? He calls it the place where they had eaten the bread and the Lord had given thanks. Now I think, on one hand, he is setting us up for the crowd's unbelief. The true redemptive-historical significance of what took place on the other side of the lake was lost on the crowd. It almost reads as if it was just another ordinary meal preceded by another ordinary prayer by the ordinary son of Joseph and Mary (v. 42).

And yet this is not an incidental aside. Verse 23 is the first time in John's Gospel that Jesus is called "The Lord." He has been called "Rabbi" by Nicodemus and "sir" by the woman at the well, but when

---

[4] Mathison, *Given For You*, 222.

[5] My reading of the text has been heavily influenced by Robert Letham's excellent book, *The Lord's Supper* (Phillipsburg NJ: Presbyterian and Reformed; 2001), 7-15.

[6] The one thing from the upper room that is missing in chapter 6 is the action of breaking bread.

John looks back at the feeding of the 5,000, he calls him Lord. There is also this matter of the Lord giving thanks. Obviously this isn't about proper manners. The Lord had *"Eucharisteō."* This is the Greek word from which we get the word "Eucharist." Your Bible might have a heading over verse 22 that says something like "The Bread of Life." That is the discussion that takes place and if you skim vv. 31-51, bread is the issue. But then there is a surprising addition in v. 53 that almost comes out of nowhere:

> [53] So Jesus said to them, "Truly, truly, I say to you, unless you eat the flesh of the Son of Man and drink his blood, you have no life in you.

Why is the *blood* of Christ introduced? This discussion was about bread, not blood, but Jesus now speaks of eating his flesh and drinking his blood. And that isn't all. John says that once the crowd heard him talking about chewing his flesh and drinking his blood, people started to leave. "After this many of his disciples turned back and no longer walked with him" (v. 66). Isn't that what happened on the night in which Jesus was betrayed? (Mk. 14:27-28). Didn't Jesus' disciples turn back from following him as they fled from Gethsemane? Jesus' final words are also highly significant:

> [70] Jesus answered them, "Did I not choose you, the Twelve? And yet one of you is a devil." [71] He spoke of Judas the son of Simon Iscariot for he, one of the Twelve, was going to betray him. (Jn. 5:70-71)

Summary

Now when we put all these pieces of chapter 6 together, a certain picture emerges. The Passover feast is at hand. Jesus shares a meal which begins with his giving thanks, and he gives the disciples bread. He declares that they must eat his flesh and drink his blood. Many disciples turn away and refuse to follow him, and Judas is identified as the betrayer. I ask you, what picture comes to your mind? This sounds like the institution of the Lord's Supper. The correspondence between the feeding of the 5,000 and the institution of the Lord's Supper in the upper room is striking. Understandably, the Reformed catechisms and confessions cite John 6 to expound the meaning of the Lord's Supper. The apostle John is not giving us his version of the Lord's Supper, but what he is giving us is the meaning of the Lord's Supper, the meaning behind the sacrament.

Several questions come to mind: What is the bread of life? Second, what does this bread of life do? Third, how do we eat the bread of life?

Bread from heaven

Jesus said to them, "I am the bread of life" (v. 35). This is the first of seven "I am" sayings in John's Gospel: I am the bread of life; I am the light of the world (8:12) ; I am the gate (10:7); I am the good shepherd (10:11) ; I am the resurrection and the life (11:25); I am the way the truth and the life (14:6) and I am the true vine (15:1,5).

And there is one more "I am" saying that was the most controversial of them all:

> [56] Your father Abraham rejoiced that he would see my day. He saw it and was glad." [57] So the Jews said to him, "You are not yet fifty years old, and have you seen Abraham?" [58] Jesus said to them, "Truly, truly, I say to you, before Abraham was, I am." [59] So they picked up stones to throw at him, but Jesus hid himself and went out of the temple. (Jn. 8:56-59)

They tried to crush the bread of life with stones. They tried to extinguish the light of the world. They tried to remove the way, silence the truth, and end the life. But Jesus is the great *I Am* who revealed himself to Moses in the burning bush. He is the Lord of the covenant, and he is the one of whom the covenant speaks.

What are we to make of Jesus as the bread of life, particularly as it relates to the Lord's Supper? Is the bread in the Lord's Supper transformed into the real, physical body of Christ so that he becomes the bread? Does the wine become his blood? This is far from the truth. Jesus is no more a piece of bread than he is a wooden gate or a grape vine. Clearly he is not saying he is physical bread, nor that the bread on the Communion table magically becomes his physical body. He is making a statement from which people are to draw a comparison.

Jesus has fed 5,000 people on five loaves of bread and two fish, and that is an incredible miracle. Yet these same people come saying, "You are going to have to prove yourself. You are going to have to do more than miraculously feed us a meal. Moses gave our fathers bread for forty years. What can you give us in comparison?" The first thing that Jesus gives them is a history lesson. The crowds must be corrected because Moses didn't feed them manna from heaven, God did. God provided bread in the wilderness, not Moses. If only God can provide bread in the wilderness and if Jesus provides it for them on the mountainside, then we must believe that he is God.

They said to him, "Lord, give us this bread always" (v. 34). They are thinking primarily in earthly terms. They failed to see how heaven is brought to earth in the person of Jesus Christ. Leon Morris writes:

> Like the woman at the well who wanted the living water these people want the bread of God... She had wanted the water to be relieved of the task of drawing [water] from the well. They had been fed from the loaves, and they probably wanted some permanent gift of this kind. And they, like her, were ironical. They did not really think that He could provide this bread.[7]

They were searching for the wrong thing. They were settling for the temporal, but what Christ offered them was eternal, and they wouldn't have it. "I am the bread of life." The life-giving bread is none other than the life-giving Jesus. They were after the wrong thing.

What does this bread of life do?

Jesus said to them, "I am the bread of life; whoever comes to me shall not hunger, and whoever believes in me shall never thirst" (v. 35).

In a word, Jesus satisfies. He is the answer to every longing, and what he is saying is he is the only one who can fill the famine that exists in your soul. Nothing else will do. Therefore, do not live your life for bread that will not satisfy; Jesus will satisfy your hunger. Dr. Derek Thomas spoke of a very famous author named Jack Higgins. He is a multi-millionaire and one of those individuals who has what it takes to get anything he wants. Well, almost anything. He was once asked if there was anything he wished he would have known about early on in life. He answered, "I wish someone had told me that when you get to the top, there's nothing there."[8]

The world said, "Get to the top and find satisfaction." He made it to the top and says, "But there is nothing here!" He knows, he's there, and he says it is empty! Put the life of money, fame, power, and ease of living alongside the poorest man who has Christ and tell me, who is the beggar? Who is the poor man? Jesus said, "Come to me and you will never hunger or thirst again."

This bread of life satisfies, and Jesus, the bread of life, sustains and nourishes us

Bread is a staple food found all around the world. We Americans love to eat. Our strength depends upon getting it. You can eat three healthy meals every day for a year, and then you come down with a stomach bug and can't eat anything for several days. How strong are you then? Your body can dip into the reserves that have been stored up, but you will not

---

[7] Leon Morris, *The Gospel According to John*, NICNT (Grand Rapids: Eerdmans; 1995), 365.

[8] Preached at First Presbyterian Church, Jackson MS.

have the strength that you previously had until you start eating regularly. We need food to grow healthy and strong, and we need food to stay healthy and strong.

When Jesus says, "I am the bread of life," he is helping us to see that he is absolutely necessary in sustaining our Christian life. When we come to church to hear the word preached and to partake of the Lord's Table, we are eating and drinking to the nourishment of our souls.[9] Jesus' body and blood are for our souls what food and drink are for our bodies. Would we really want to only infrequently experience that which Jesus says we desperately need? The covenant Lord provides his covenant people with spiritual life and nourishment.

How do we eat of it?

Jesus has promised to do all these things, so then, how do we "eat" him? How do we eat his flesh and drink his blood seeing that Jesus is in heaven? Jesus then said to them, "Truly, truly, I say to you, it was not Moses who gave you the bread from heaven, but my Father gives you the true bread from heaven" (v. 32). If we are going to have this living bread, God must give him. It is the Father who gives the Son, and by the Spirit of God we feast on Christ and his benefits. It is the will and work of God to strengthen his people's faith through this meal. We come to the table believing, which is a gift of God, and God strengthens that faith by his Spirit, who raises us up to commune with the resurrected and glorified Christ (1 Cor. 10:16). God gives; we receive. That is what Jesus is teaching the crowds here. And is this not what takes place in the Lord's Supper? When he had given thanks, he broke it and said, "This is my body which is given for you, do this in remembrance of me" (1 Cor. 11:24). We receive the symbols of his body and blood and with the mouth of faith we "spiritually, receive, and feed upon, Christ crucified,

---

[9] Why then does Christ call the bread his body and the cup his blood, or the new covenant in his blood? (Paul uses the words, a participation in Christ's body and blood.) Christ has good reason for these words. He wants to teach us that as bread and wine nourish our temporal life, so too his crucified body and poured-out blood truly nourish our souls for eternal life. But more important, he wants to assure us, by this visible sign and pledge, that we, through the Holy Spirit's work, share in his true body and blood as surely as our mouths receive these holy signs in his remembrance, and that all of his suffering and obedience are as definitely ours as if we personally had suffered and paid for our sins. (Heidelberg Catechism Lord's Day 29, Q/A 79)

and all benefits of His death: the body and blood of Christ."[10] In the words of the Westminster Larger Catechism 62, the benefits of Christ for the believer "strengthen and increase their faith, and all other graces." The Lord not only gives us the benefits of what Jesus has done; he gives us his Son:

> [16] And I will ask the Father, and he will give you another Helper, to be with you forever, [17] even the Spirit of truth, whom the world cannot receive, because it neither sees him nor knows him. You know him, for he dwells with you and will be in you. [18] "I will not leave you as orphans; I will come to you. [19] Yet a little while and the world will see me no more, but you will see me. Because I live, you also will live. [20] In that day you will know that I am in my Father, and you in me, and I in you. (Jn. 14:16-20)

We live, because he lives. Our life is united to Christ's life. He lives forever, so we too will live forever and though we die, yet we live (Jn. 11:25). But the union is more than just standing side-by-side with Jesus. Jesus said, "I am *in* my Father, and you are *in* me," and then note those final words, *"and I in you."* [11]

Since he promises to feed our souls with the life-giving body and blood of Christ Jesus, he will certainly do it. I would also add here that he does it whether or not we feel it in any sort of subjective way. When we eat and drink, we do not always feel the benefit that our body derives from it, but we really and truly receive the benefits of it. So also in the

---

[10] Westminster Confession of Faith 29.7.

[11] "Now, as it is certain and beyond all doubt that Jesus Christ has not enjoined to us the use of His sacraments in vain, so He works in us all that He represents to us by these holy signs, though the manner surpasses our understanding and cannot be comprehended by us, as the operations of the Holy Spirit are hidden and incomprehensible. In the meantime we err not when we say that what is eaten and drunk by us is the proper and natural body and the proper blood, of Christ. But the manner of our partaking of the same is not by the mouth, but by the spirit through faith. Thus, then, though Christ always sits at the right hand of His Father in the heavens, yet does He not therefore cease to make us partakers of Himself by faith. This feast is a spiritual table, at which Christ communicates Himself with all His benefits to us, and gives us there to enjoy both Himself and the merits of His sufferings and death: nourishing, strengthening, and comforting our poor comfortless souls by the eating of His flesh, quickening and refreshing them by the drinking of His blood." Belgic Confession, Article 35.

Lord's Supper, the Lord is sovereignly working through the sacrament, the benefit of which is beyond our finite minds to comprehend or our senses to measure.

From hillside to upper room

The sacrament is that regular, perpetual feast, and this feast of bread and wine transcends those that came before it. In the upper room, Jesus celebrated the Passover with his disciples. They reclined at the table; they ate lamb and bitter herbs; they drank wine and commemorated the night in which God redeemed his people from Egypt. The sword of the destroyer had entered the houses of the Egyptians, but the Israelites were spared because blood of sacrificial lambs was smeared across their doorposts. The lambs that were slain and applied to the Israelite houses sealed them off from the angel of death. On that night, they obtained their freedom to go and worship God and to finally enter into his covenant at the mountain. Little did the disciples know that the rite of Passover was passing away in the presence of the Lamb.

As the night wore on, Jesus took bread and when he had given thanks, he broke it and gave it to them, saying, "This is my body, which is given for you. Do this in remembrance of me" (Lk. 22:19). What happened next could not be easily forgotten. Jesus took the glass of wine and said, "This cup that is poured out for you is the new covenant in my blood" (v. 20). This was an astounding claim. At the foot of Mount Sinai, Moses sprinkled the people with blood and said, "Behold the blood of the covenant that the Lord has made with you in accordance with all these words" (Ex. 24:8). That covenant, that relationship between God and his people, was repeatedly broken by God's friends. A broken covenant, forged under pain of death, required that their blood be spilled. But Jesus declared a new covenant which was enacted by his blood. No longer would there be any need for the blood of animals to be shed because the blood of the Lamb of God covered all for whom he died. The destroyer could not turn his sword against them because on this night, Christ would leave the house to face him on their behalf.

At the Last Supper, Jesus showed himself to be the covenant Lord and gave them the new sign of the new covenant. In the Old Testament it was God who gave Israel the covenant signs. By giving a new sign of the new covenant, Jesus revealed his divine identity. By calling attention to his own blood of the covenant, he calls for us to stand at the cross in holy wonder as the covenant Lord becomes the covenant sacrifice.

Connecting the old covenants to the new sign

Now it becomes crystal clear that Adam's sin brought death, but the covenant Lord promised life. The striking of the deal is the ransom to be paid for sin's wage, and Jesus paid it all. Noah crossed the waters of judgment through a wooden boat and would himself be carried through the flood of judgment by Jesus crucified upon a wooden cross (Gal. 2:20; Col. 3:3). God walked the path of blood in Abraham's day which was a path that would bring a bloodied Jesus to the cross. Israel swore allegiance to the covenant, but they didn't remain faithful and were cast out of the land of Canaan. Jesus' obedience to all that God commanded satisfied the rights to an eternal inheritance of a heavenly land that could never be lost by the disobedience of the heirs of this new covenant (Rev. 21-22). By his blood that was shed, our faces are sprinkled clean (Rev. 1:5). David's sons were punished with the stripes of man (2 Sam. 7:14; Matt. 27:26), and for a time God's steadfast love departed from him (2 Sam. 7:15; Mk. 15:33-34) as the sins of his people were placed upon him. He was placed in a tomb, but after three days he took his place among the living never to die again. God raised him up and exalted him as king over all, seating him upon the throne of David (Lk. 1:32; Acts 2:30; Heb. 1:8). And from this king's heavenly table, he gives us his resurrected life as food and drink for our souls. This new covenant produced in his people a new heart, with new obedience because of a new reality—sins remembered no more (Heb. 8:12-13) because God remembered the new covenant and sent his Son to secure this new life we enjoy, in the new covenant he made, through his broken body and shed blood.

Study Questions:

1. What is the symbolism of bread and wine?
2. Why does Christ command us to eat his flesh and drink his blood? How do we do that?
3. What does the Spirit do through the Lord's Supper?
4. How can we foster both serious reflection and joyfulness at the Lord's Table?

Bibliography

Alexander, T. Desmond., and Brian Rosner S. *New Dictionary of Biblical Theology*. Leicester, England: Inter-Varsity, 2000.

Alexander, T. Desmond, and Baker, David W. *Dictionary of the Old Testament: Pentateuch*. Downers Grove, IL: Inter-Varsity Press, 2003.

Arnold, Bill. *1 & 2 Samuel*. Grand Rapids: Zondervan, 2003.

Bavinck, H., John Bolt, and John Vriend. *Reformed Dogmatics*. Grand Rapids, MI: Baker Academic, 2008.

Beale, G. K. *The Temple and the Church's Mission: A Biblical Theology of the Dwelling Place of God*. Downers Grove, IL: Apollos, 2004.

Beale, G. K. *A New Testament Biblical Theology: The Unfolding of the Old Testament in the New*. Grand Rapids, MI: Baker Academic, 2011.

Brueggemann, Walter. *Genesis*. Atlanta: Westminster John Knox Press, 1982.

Buchanan, James. *The Doctrine of Justification: An Outline of its History in the Church and of its Exposition from Scripture*. Carlisle: The Banner of Truth Trust, 1991.

Calvin, John. *Commentaries on the Prophet Jeremiah and the Lamentations*. Grand Rapids: Baker, 2003.

Calvin, John. *Commentary on Timothy, Titus, Philemon*. Grand Rapids: Baker, 2003.

Calvin, John. *Institutes of the Christian Religion*. 2 vols. Trans. F. L. Battles, ed. J. T. McNeill. Philadelphia: Westminster, 1960.

Carson, Donald A. *Right with God. Justification in the Bible and the World*. Carlisle: Paternoster; Grand Rapids: Baker, 1992.

Collins, C. John. *Genesis 1-4: A Linguistic, Literary, and Theological Commentary*. Phillipsburg, NJ: P & R Pub., 2006.

Estelle, Bryan D., J. Fesko V., and David VanDrunen. *The Law Is Not of Faith: Essays on Works and Grace in the Mosaic Covenant*. Phillipsburg, NJ: P & R Pub., 2009.

Fisher, Edward, and Thomas Boston. *The Marrow of Modern Divinity*. Ross-shire, Scotland: Christian Focus Publications, 2009.

Gentry, Peter J., and Wellum, Stephen J. *Kingdom Through Covenant: A Biblical Theological Understanding of the Covenants*. Wheaton: Crossway, 2012.

Goldsworthy, Graham. *Preaching the Whole Bible As Christian Scripture*. Grand Rapids: Eerdmans, 2000.

Henry, Matthew. *Matthew Henry's Commentary on the Whole Bible, Isaiah to Malachi*. New York: Fleming H Revel, n.d.

Heppe, Heinrich, and Ernst Bizer. *Reformed Dogmatics*. London: Wakeman Trust, 2002.

Hess, Richard S., and Tsumura, David Toshio. *I Studied Inscriptions from Before the Flood:Ancient Near Eastern, Literary, and Linguistic Approaches to Genesis 1-11*. Winona Lake: Eisenbrauns, 1994.

Hodge, Charles. *Systematic Theology*. Grand Rapids: Eerdmans, 1997.

Horton, Michael Scott. *The Christian Faith: A Systematic Theology for Pilgrims on the Way*. Grand Rapids, MI: Zondervan, 2011.

Horton, Michael Scott. *God of Promise: Introducing Covenant Theology*. Grand Rapids, MI: Baker, 2006.

Johnson, Dennis E. *Him We Proclaim: Preaching Christ from All the Scriptures*. Phillipsburg, NJ: P&R Pub., 2007.

Kidner, Derek. *Genesis, Tyndale Old Testament Commentary*. Downers Grove, IL: Inter-Varsity Press, 1967.

Kline, Meredith G. *By Oath Consigned*. Grand Rapids: Eerdmans, 1968.

Bibliography

Kline, Meredith G., *Kingdom Prologue*. South Hamilton, MA: self published, 1993.

Letham, Robert. *The Lord's Supper: Eternal Word in Broken Bread*. Phillipsburg, NJ: P & R Pub., 2001.

Mathison, Keith A. *Given for You: Reclaiming Calvin's Doctrine of the Lord's Supper*. Phillipsburg, NJ: P&R Pub., 2002.

McKeown, James. *Genesis, The Two Horizons Old Testament Commentary*. Grand Rapids/Cambridge: Eerdmans, 2008.

Morris, Leon. *The Gospel According to John*. NICNT. Grand Rapids: Eerdmans, 1995.

Peterson, David G. *Transformed by God: New Covenant Life and Ministry*. Downers Grove: Inter-Varisty Press., 2012.

Pink, Arthur W. *Genesis*. Chicago: Moody, 1922.

Robertson, O Palmer. *The Christ of the Covenants*. Phillipsburg, NJ: P&R Pub., 1980.

Robertson, O Palmer. *Covenants: God's Way With His People*. Suwanee: Great Commission Publications, 2003.

Ryken, T. Leland, Wilhoit, James C., and Longman, Tremper III. *Dictionary of Biblical Imagery*. Leicester: Inter-Varsity Press, 1998.

Sailhamer, John. *The Pentateuch as Narrative: A Biblical-theological Commentary*. Grand Rapids, MI: Zondervan, 1992. Print.

Sproul, R. C. *Essential Truths of the Christian Faith*. Wheaton: Tyndale House, 1992.

Stonehouse, Ned B. *J. Gresham Machen: A Biographical Memoir*. Carlisle: Banner of Truth, 1977.

Turretin, Francis, George Giger Musgrave., and James Dennison T. *Institutes of Elenctic Theology*. Phillipsburg, NJ: P&R Pub., 1992.

Vos, Geerhardus., and Danny Olinger. *A Geerhardus Vos Anthoogy*. Philipsburg, NJ: P&R Pub., 2005.

Waltke, Bruce K., and Charles Yu. *An Old Testament Theology: An Exegetical, Canonical, and Thematic Approach*. Grand Rapids: Zondervan, 2007.

Warfield, Benjamin B. *Selected Shorter Writings of Benjamin B. Warfield*. Phillipsburg, NJ: P&R Pub., 1970.

Wenham, Gordon. *Word Biblical Commentary, Vol. 1: Genesis 1-15*. Nashville: Thomas Nelson, 1987.

Williamson, Paul R. *Sealed with an Oath: Covenant in God's Unfolding Purpose*. Downers Grove, IL: Apollos/InterVarsity, 2007.

Witsius, Herman. The Economy of the Covenants Between God and Man. Phillipsburg, NJ: P&R Pub., 1990.

Scripture Index

Genesis

1	23, 27, 38, 43, 45, 49		53, 59, 66, 85, 89, 99, 102, 133
1:2	45	3:18	78
1:22	69	3:19	24
1:26–30	77	3:20	31
1:27	21	3:21	77
1:28	23	3:22	18
1:31	38	3:24	21, 28
1–3	17, 19	4	36, 134
1–4	5, 148	4:13	36
		4:14	37
1–11	20, 148	4:15	35
1–15	27, 41, 150	4:23	38
2	18, 26, 27, 53	4:30	134
		5	51
2:2–3	82	5:1–3	69, 87
2:7	18, 24	5:4	51
2:8	20	5:29	41
2:9	18	6	39, 51
2:10–14	20	6:2–3	37, 51
2:15	21, 78	6:5, 11	38
2:15–17	27	6:5–8	38
2:17	17, 18, 22, 28, 69	6:8	35, 39
3	22, 28, 29, 33, 53	6:9	35, 39, 53
		6:11	41
3:1	27	6:13	35
3:1–6	26	6:14	40
3:6	53	6:15	40
		6:16	40
3:12	78	6:18	42, 44
3:14	29	6:22	35, 40, 41, 53
3:15	7, 30, 31, 35, 36, 46, 47, 49, 50,	7	41, 43, 134
		7:1	35, 134

Reference	Page(s)
7:1, 4	43
7:2, 8	41
7:5	40
7:7	35
7:11	43
7:11–24	123
7:17	43
7:21–23	43
7–8	99
8:1	45
8:13	41
8:18	53
8:21	39
8:21–22	35
8:22	45
9	35
9:1	51
9:11	35
9:16	46
10:5	52
10:18	52
10:20	52
10:31	52
10:32	52
11	51
11:1–9	51, 89
12	51, 118
12:1, 4	55
12:1–3	50, 52
12:2	87
12:3	52, 133
12:19	78
13	118
13:4	55
13:10	53, 56, 78
13:15	56
14	55
15	54, 59, 60, 99, 116, 118
15:1	55, 60
15:1–3	54
15:2	60
15:2–3	55
15:4	60, 85
15:5	55
15:6	57, 60, 128
15:7	60
15:9–11	57
15:14	60
15:16	116
15:17–18	59
15:18	56, 60
16	53
16:3	54
17	128
17:4–6	133
17:6	51
17:7, 10	127
17:7–8	87
17:9–13	130
17:9–14	128
17:10	5
17:15	55
17:18–19, 23	130
19	44
19:29	44
21:4	130
21:12	87
22:17	87
22:18	87
26	87
26:24	87
28:12	89
30	44
30:20	44
38	53

49:8–12	85	24:3	78
		24:7	99
Exodus		24:8	115, 119, 145
1:5–22	114		
1:7	69, 114, 118	25, 1	40
		25:10–22	90
1:8	114	25:11	40
1:8–14	114, 118	25:18	82
2	44, 114, 119	26	41
		26:14	41
2:24	44	26–27	40
3	119	29:42–46	90
3:13–15	9	32	115, 119
4:1–9	114	32:13	115
4:22–23	69, 87, 114	32:31–32	128
4–12	114, 119	32:32	118
6:2–4	27	34	115, 119
12	114, 119	34:29–35	115
12:11	5	34:35	119
12:22	114	37:2	40
12:25–27	128	40:16	41
12:29	119	40:34–35	90
12:29–30	114		
13:5	67	**Leviticus**	
13:18	114	11	41
14	114, 119	16	134
16	115, 119	16:6, 11	134
19	60, 69, 115, 119	16:24	65
		18:5	18, 69, 100
19	69	18:26–28	71
19:5	69, 75, 76, 102	20:22	71
		23:39–43	66
19:7–8	69	26:22	72
19:18	60		
20	115, 119	**Numbers**	
20:2	65	3	22, 41
20:18	115	3:7–8	22
20–23	70	3:25	41
22:24	72	7:89	82, 90

8:24–27	21	30:19	69, 72
11:29	13	30:20	72
12	87	32:43	111
12:7	87	33:7	60
13	119	33:9	60
13:2	115	33:21	60
14	87, 115	33:22	60
14:1–11	119	33:23	60
14:24	87	33:28	60
14:26	119	33:29	60
14:26–38	115		
14:34	115, 119	**Joshua**	
14:39	115	1	116, 119
20:8, 11–12	48	2	119
		2:1	116
Deuteronomy		3	116, 120
4:25–26	70	4	134
4:40	72	4:15	134
6	134	5	116, 120
6:22	134	6–11	120
11:11	123	23:14	92, 116
11:18	102	24:15	131
11:19–21	72		
12:1–9	90	**Judges**	
12:5	82	10:6	90
12:25, 28	72		
16	82	**1 Samuel**	
16:2, 6–7	82	1	44, 134
18:15–19	7	1:19	44
18:18	65	1:21	134
27–28	97	4:4	90
28:1–2	18	13:14	80
28:36, 63–68	101		
29:9	100	**2 Samuel**	
30	71	5:6–7	86
30:6	65, 129	5:7	80
30:14	102	5:7–9	82
30:17–20	71	5:10	86

6	82	8:5	78
6:12–16	82	19:11	18
6:16	82	22:1	47
7	88	33:11	15
7:1	82, 86	46:3	123
7:2	84	51:1–9	106
7:5–7	84	58:11	18
7:8–14	88	79:3	101
7:9	87	89:23	87
7:11	87	89:26	87
7:12	84, 85, 88	97	111
7:13	85	103:2–4	74
7:14	87, 91, 93, 146	110	106
		119:165	74
7:15	146	132:7–8	82
7:16	85, 90		
7:18	88	**Isaiah**	
7:24	87	2:2–4	90
9	134	2:3	89
9:9	134	9:6–7	7
22	83	13	123
22:21–24	83	13:6, 9	123
		14:24	3
1 Chronicles		25:8	48
17:13	111	32:17–18	48
23	22	40:3	121
23:32	22	42:6	15
		44:3	123
Ezra		46:10	15
		51:2	128
3:10	80	53	106
		53:5–6	93
Nehemiah		53:10	9
9:15	123, 154	54:9–10	49
		61:6	76
		63:16	128
Psalms		65:25	42
2	111	66:18	9
7:11–12	35		

Jeremiah

2:2	101
2:8	105
2:20	101
2:23–24	101
5:1, 5	104
5:4	105
5:5	105
8:7	105
9:3	105
9:6	105
14:10	106
17	102
17:1	102
24:7	103, 105
31	8, 98
31:31, 33	99
31:32	100
31:33	102, 103
31:34	106
34	3, 58
34 f	58
34:15	58
34:16	59
34:17–20	59
38	134
38:17	134
46	123
46:10	123

Ezekiel

16:1–6	67
40–48	40
44	22
44:14	22
47	20

Hosea

6:7	71
11:1	69

Joel

1	123
1:15	123
2:3	69
2:28	13

Amos

1:1–15	90
5	123
5:18–21	123

Obadiah

1	123
1:15	123

Micah

4:1–3	90

Zephaniah

1	123
1:14–18	123

Zechariah

6:12–13	7

Malachi

2:14	5
4	123
4:5	123

Matthew

1:1	31, 109, 116, 118
1:1ff	61
1:2, 6, 16	116
1:2–17	118
1:18–25	119

2:13–14	119	22	84
2:14	116	22:30	23
2:16–18	118	22:44–45	84
3	123	23:36	119
3:2, 7–10	116	24:2	117
3:8	122	24:34	119
3:9	122	25:34	110
3:10	122	26	119, 120
3:11	122	26:26–28	5
3:12	122	26:28	117
3:13	78	26:33	118
3:13–17	116, 119, 120	27:26	146
		27:29	78
3:14	123	27:45, 51–53	118
3:15	123	27:45–46	93
3:17	77, 116	27:50	119
4:1	117	28:1–10	119
4:1–11	119	28:19	5, 118, 120, 124, 128
4:6	32		
4:10	32	52–53	119
5:17	102		
5:45	35	**Luke**	
5–7	117, 119	3	37
8:11	86	3:38	37, 87
8–9	119		
10	119	**John**	
11	123	1:3	110
11:2–3	123	1:14	9
12:38	117	2	86
13:24–30	105	3	103
13:30	42	3:5–8	48
14:13–20	119	4:34	15
15:29 ff	119	5	112
17:1–8	119	5:46	8, 118
17:6	117	5:70–71	140
19:16–17	18	6	138, 139, 140
20:28	110		
21–25	119	6:4	139

6:22–23	139	2:28–29	129
6:38	15	4	83
8:44	36	4:6	83
8:56–59	141	4:6–10	129
9:4	15	4:25	123
10:18	15	5	23, 29
10:29	15	5:12–14	72
11:25	144	5:12ff	19
12:21	110	5:13	106
13:36	99	5:14	8, 72, 83, 109
14:1–3	9		
14:16–20	144	5:14 ff.	69
14:20	138	6:1–5	48
17:4	15	6:1–11	121
17:23	138	6:3	127
17:24	9	6:4	125
19:4	93	6:5	124
19:24	77	6:23	72
19:30	15, 47, 78	7	89
		7:15, 19	89
Acts		8:3	100
1:8	13	8:31	45
1:9	9	9:16	126
2:29–36	95	9:31–33	64
2:30	146	10:5	18
2:37–39	132	11:16–17	133
2:38–39	133		
2:39	127		
2:41	124		
3:22	80	**1 Corinthians**	
7:8	130	1:10–17	127
13:22	93	2	14
13:32–37	94	3:16–17	48, 99
		6:11	14, 127
Romans		6:19	48
1:1–4	93	10:2	115
1:1–6	85	10:16	143
1:3	87	10:16–17	124
2:4	35	11:24	143

12:13	127	2:19–22	48
15	23, 24	4:11–12	104
15:22	29	4:24	5
15:44	23		
15:45	19, 47	**Philippians**	
15:45–47	24	3:3	128

2 Corinthians

2	48	**Colossians**	
3:6	99	1:16	110
5:17	110	2:11–12	129
6:16	48	2:11–13	126, 129
		2:12	124, 129
		2:17	8
Galatians		3:1–3	48
2:16	128	3:3	146
2:20	146		
3:6–7	64	**1 Timothy**	
3:13	73, 93	1:8	73
3:16	61, 81, 92		
3:16, 26–29	99	**Hebrews**	
3:17	101	1:1	68
		1:1–4	111
3:18	81	1:8	146
3:18–19	106	2:10	iii
3:26–29	61	4:10–11	82
3:27	124	4:15	9
3:29	128, 130, 133	7	106
		7:12	106
4:4	9, 109	7:14–16	94
4:24–26	129	7:18	106
		7:22	106
Ephesians		7:26–28	48
1	1, 126	7–10	106
1:4	11	8:5	25
1:7	12	8:6	iii, 107
1:13–14	13	8:6–8, 13	100
2:9–22	95	8:10, 12	89
2:12–18	99	8:12–13	146
2:15	133	8:13	107

9:11	106	**1 John**	
9:13–14	106	2:16	104
9:15	56, 128		
9:15	106	**Revelation**	
9:15–16	106	1:5	146
10	14	2:7	89
10:3	106	2:10	89
10:4	106	5:6	9
10:5–7	15	21	24, 40
10:5–10	14	21:1–3	24
10:12	107	21:2, 9	124
		21:6	89
10:14	106	21–22	48, 56, 146
10:19–20	8	22:1–3	21
10:19–25	107		
10:22	106		
11	80		
11:7	40		
11:10	56		
11:10–16	92		
11:13–16	56		
11:15–16	56		
12:22	80		
10, 14			

1 Peter
1:5	13
1:20	15
2:24	32
3:20–21	99
3:21	83, 123

2 Peter
2:5	42, 47
3:5–7	34, 35
3:13	48

www.ingramcontent.com/pod-product-compliance
Lightning Source LLC
LaVergne TN
LVHW051601070426
835507LV00021B/2703